AF612215

LEARNING TECHNOLOGY CHANGES HUMAN LEISURE BEHAVIOR

JOHN LOK

Contents

Preface

Introduction

In global service industry, entertainment industry has high market share in overall industries. entertainment industry may include: hotel, tourism, movie, music, sport, publishing, electronic playing game etc. these main several aspects. Human must need any kinds of entertainment, for example, liking reading people who must go to book stores or enter e-publishing stores to buy any paper books or e-books to read. Otherwise, like sport or enjoyment tourism people, who must choose to spend time to play any football, basketball or swimming etc. different kinds of sports or going to travel agents to pay money to buy air tickets to choose anywhere to travel.

Hence, due to human needs any kinds of entertainment to enjoy our lives, instead of working. If any entertainment businessmen can predict whether what factors will influence general entertainment consumers' entertainment choices change as well as they can predict why and how their entertainment consumption of kinds change. Then, their entertainment businesses can have much accurate prediction to any kinds of entertainment consumers' behaviors.

This book explain some psychological concept to analyze why and how the different kinds of entertainment consumers' entertainment needs how brings economic growth. In my this book, I shall attempt to explain how and why ecommerce may be one kind network human job. Also, I shall indicate reasons to explain why human network behavior may bring direct or indirect influences to economy growth or recession in our global societies in macro and micro economy view. Why leisure changing environment may influence human behavior , even economic environment changes. I shall indicate cases to explain any possible human social activities may bring direct or indirect influences to cause our social economic growth or recession in consequency in possible. I hope that my readers can feel more understanding whether what real meaning of behavioral economy is the relationship between our behaviors and our economy.

Prologue

Table of content

CHAPTER I

Sport industry entertainment consumer pscyhology

Nowadays, the sports business industry is made up of establishments and the employees of corporations who are primarily concerned with aspects of sports having to do with management, marketing, economics, and finance, amongst other venues. The sports business industry focuses on the sports themselves, as well as the place of sports in society, and the principles that support the sporting industry. The sports business industry is involved in the merger between sports and business, and how these fields work interactively for mutual benefits and profitability.

The sports business industry is interdisciplinary and may involved planning sporting events and effectively marketing for sports, as well as working with accounting, communications, law, and psychology skills. The sports business industry tackles the development of risk management plans for any legal issues that may occur, the negotiations of contracts for players in the industry, and/or strategies for effective media relations.

In fact, instead of sport indutry may include any kinds of sports, e.g. swimming, football, basketball, table tennis, tennis, riding bicycle, climbing, running etc. different kinds of sports to let young and old people enjoy lives. When they play any kinds of sports, they must need to spend some money to any any kinds of sport tools, e.g. swimming pool, table tennis hand tools, bicyle , football, basketball etc. sport useful tools. So, if any one kinds of sport industry can develop in good suitation, then it can influence the sport related useful products sale number because when the sport entertainment player chooses to spend time to play the kind of sport, then the kind of sport sports need be influenced to rise needs. So, if the kind of sport is popular, then the kind of sport product will also influenced to rise needs. So, how to develop the kind of sport in order to attract global sport entertainment players to choose to play the kind of sport, this sport development factor will influence the kind of sport need or innovative development and its related sport products useful tool need increases globally.

- How legalization impacts sports betting economics

A closer look at factors shaping the future of online sports . For example, Americans place $50 billion to $60 billion a year in illegal sports bets, dwarfing the legal $5 billion in Nevada sports betting. This represents a potentially enormous market now that states can decide whether to legalize sports gambling. Although exciting, uncertainties remain that will impact industry size, scale, and opportunity moving forward.The current state of sports gambling. In the immediate US the Supreme Court's decision to overturn the Professional and Amateur Sports Protection Act (PASPA) in May 2018, some states scrambled to pursue a lucrative opportunity independently, without a federal framework in place. Delaware and New Jersey, the plaintiff of the Supreme Court Case (Murphy vs. NCAA), were the first to act and have seen major returns, with more than $385 million a month being wagered in New Jersey alone. Eight states have currently legalized sports gambling, with more to potentially follow in short order as bills are reviewed by state legislatures. These near-term developments will be interesting to watch as sportsbooks lobby for legalization on the state level.The federal government is attempting to secure a wider blanket agreement on the federal level to protect public welfare and the integrity of the game, and generate sufficient tax revenue. The leagues support a federal framework because it can address their interests on a national level. The sportsbooks would prefer legislation that mirrors the way gambling is currently regulated on the state level by the Nevada State Gaming Commission. This situation, like many legalization efforts, is extremely fluid and will change rapidly as the critical uncertainties mentioned below unfold. Depending on the outcome, companies that are able to get in on sports betting could realize a substantial payout.

Hence, global sport entertainment poduct merchants or suppliers, they must need to know how to avoid the illegal sport products can be sold from internet or online channel to enter the kind of sport product market to compete to them illegally any time. Due to ecommerce is popular , so it influences many sport entertainment products consumers may choose to buy any kinds of sport products from online in preference. So, they can not neglect these illegal sport entertainment product sellers' sale behaviors from internet any time.

For US sport industry development example, economists estimate the economic scope of the sports industry in the United States. Drawing on a variety of data sources, they investigate the economic size of sport participation, sports viewing, and the supply and demand side of the sports market in the United States. Estimates of the size of the sports industry based on aggregate demand and aggregate supply range from $44 to $73 billion in 2005. In addition, participation in sports and the opportunity time cost of attending sporting events are important, but hard to value, components of the industry

Sport is a complex, multi-faceted activity encompassing modern spectacles like the Summer and Winter Olympic games and informal pick-up games on urban basketball courts; a recreational jogger, a runner in the Boston Marathon – a competition with thousands of participants -- and people watching the Boston Marathon on television all participate in sport in some way. So, such as Boston Marathon sport game example, if it can provide good sport entertainement show to let global sport auidence to feel exciting and visable enjoyment. Then, the year Boston Marathon competitive game can help advertisement industry and the tennis sport product industry increase tennis products buyer number and advertisement entertainment income and the Boston Marathon competitive game show income. So, one good sport competitive show may help the country's GDP growth, e.g. World Cup football competitive show, World Cup riding competitive show, World Cup swimming show etc. So, any countries government can not neglect how to develop and innovate and promote themselves any sport competive shows and sport entertainments in order to raise GDP growth and create more related sport occupations to reduce unemployment ratio in our nowadays society.

Relatively little attention has been paid in the past to estimating the economic scope of the sports industry, perhaps because of difficulties formulating an appropriate economic definition of sport. A sizable literature documenting the economic scope and economic impact of specific sports or sporting events, already exists, in part because of the ease of defining the limits of events like a golf tournament or season of professional baseball sport industry.

One key issue in defining sport involves identifying criteria that separate sport from games of skill like chess or poker and from recreational activities like dancing, hiking, fishing, and gardening. A secondary issue involves identifying criteria that appropriately define competition in a way to distinguish sport from exercise. For example, running has a competitive dimension but jogging does not. Note that weightlifting is an Olympic sport, bodybuilding is a professional sport, and competitions based on athletic performance on fitness equipment like stationary rowing machines, elliptical trainers and stationary bicycles exist, blurring the already murky distinction between exercise and sport.

In estimating the economic scope of the sports industry is to define the industry in economic terms. Several frameworks for defining the sports industry have been proposed; much of this research emerged from Europe, where government policymakers took an interest in estimating the overall economic importance of sport several decades ago. While a national income and product accounting approach has some appeal, because of the well-developed methodology and the existence of rich set of frequently updated accounts for many developed economies, it also has some weaknesses. First, on the national product side the analyst is at the mercy of the existing production classification system. All levels of government are involved in the provision of sports facilities and other important activities on the supply side of the sports market, and national income and product accounts do not contain detailed estimates of government spending on many specific items. Much of the activity in the sports market involves non-traded goods and labor inputs not valued at market prices, such as WORLD CUP SPORT COMPETITIVE GAME, WORLD GOLF, WOLRD TENNIS SHOW as well as any sport service workers they are needed to work in these any one big shows. Hence, the sport show audience number will influence any one these sport show income and employees number. The sport show employees needing number will depend on these activities factors , such as:

1. Activities involving participation in sport
2. Activities involving attendance at spectator sporting events
3. Activities involving following spectator sporting events through some media.

We recognize that each component contains elements that could be defined as recreation, exercise, or games of skill. For example, including participation in sport means that some activities that could be defined as exercise, like aerobics or walking, will be included in our definition. Including spectator sports means that auto racing, figure skating, and other such activities will be included in our definition.

Individuals can participate in the sport market in three ways: by participating some sport, by attending a sporting event, or by watching or listening to a sporting event on television, radio, or the internet. Each generates direct and indirect economic activity. All three take time, and economic theory tells us that time use has an opportunity cost. In this case, the opportunity cost of individual participation in sport is the value of the next best opportunity for an individual. For consumers of sport, this opportunity cost can be valued in terms of forgone wages or earnings. Furthermore, participating in sport requires equipment, fees, and potentially travel, all of which generate economic activity. Attending a sporting event involves purchasing tickets, travel and perhaps other purchases like food and souvenirs. Watching or listening to sporting events requires equipment, in the form of televisions, radios or computers, as well as subscriptions to broadcast services. Since all of these economic activities increase with the number of participants, documenting the number of participants is an important indicator of the scope of the sports market.

On conclusion, more importantly, individuals' participation in the sports market generates significant economic benefits beyond direct and indirect economic activity. Individuals derive satisfaction, or utility, from participation in the sports market, which has economic value. In economics view, individuals' participation in the sports market produces consumption benefits. These consumption benefits are not bought and sold like tickets, but they are important when assessing the overall scope of the sports market. Although placing a dollar value on sport related consumption benefits is beyond the scope of this paper, it is safe to say that the value of these consumption benefits rises with the number of participants in the sports market.

- Sport consumer behaviors

Despite the recent rapid spread of leisure involvement and loyalty research, very little attention has been given to the conceptualization of the nature of involvement's relationship with loyalty of sport fans. Whether psychological commitment and attitudinal loyalty intervene in the relationship between sport fans' involvement and their behavioral loyalty to a soccer team. For a soccer team sport competition example, it indicate that psychological commitment and attitudinal loyalty intervene in the relationship between sport fans' involvement and their behavioral loyalty to the soccer teams. It is suggested that marketing strategies may be developed to strengthen psychological commitment and attitudinal loyalty in order to maximize behavioral loyalty.

Involvement has been defined as 'a person's perceived relevance of the object based on inherent needs, values, and interests' (Zaichkowsky, 1985, p. 342). Leisure involvement refers to an unobservable state of motivation, arousal or interest toward a recreational activity or associated product that is evoked by a particular or stimulus that possesses drive properties (Iwasaki & Havitz, 1998).

So, any sport competitive show's audience , their psychological commitment factors are very important. They may include: psychological commitment ,attitudinal loyalty behavioral loyalty. For example, psychological commitment is a mediating variable between involvement and behavioral loyalty. Additionally, attitudinal loyalty is a mediating factor that facilitates the relationship between psychological commitment and behavioral loyalty. It seems that not all highly involved spectators become loyal to their team, although higher levels of enduring involvement seem to be an important precursor to behavioral loyalty. Higher levels of psychological commitment, in which attitudinal loyalty is a crucial element, appear essential for the development of spectators' behavioral loyalty to a team. The development of spectators' behavioral loyalty appears to be best explained as a progressive process in which the formation of high involvement seems to be a precondition for becoming a committed spectator of a team.

On conclusion, any sport competitive shows, how the show can influence and attract audience, the entertainment attractive factor will influence the time sport show success in sport industry long term development. So, how to develop sport entertainment show, it will be one important issue to bring any country's sport income nowadays.

- SPORT HEALTH INFLUENCES SPORT CONSUMERS NUMBER INCREASES

I beleive that when one country is experiencing stable economic growth, it will lead more healthier, I shall indicate reasons as below:

How can economic growth lead healthier to poor people? Can economic growth influence medical service quality and doctors and nurses medical service performance of hospitals? Can economic growth influence quality of medicine to let patients to eat in order to raise more healthier? Has economic growth and medical health service (production of medicine quality) direct or indirect relationship to lead patients more healthier? What are health impact income?

I assume that life expectancy will be better, if the country has better economic growth or it improves its economic growth. I shall indicate the reasons include as below:

Firstly on relationship hand , I believe that it has relationship between income and health or life expectancy hand, due to the country can develop or grow up or grow its economy to remain long term good economic development. So, its citizen can have more jobs supply to do to treat any sickness. So, they will have effort to buy different kinds of medicine to eat in order to raise more healthier. It seems that some economists support long term good economic growth will bring the country's medical development, e.g. many hospitals can have more effort money to spend to research any new kinds of medicines to let patients to choose the most health medicines to eat, when patietns have different kinds of medicines to choose to eat in order to choose to eat th enough nutrition improvement of different kinds of medicines. Then, the country's patients will have more chance to treat their sickness to be improved health.

Hence, it seems that hospitals will have enough money to research ,when the country has long term better economic growth condition. When the country can remain long term better environment growth improvement, it can lead many jobs to be supplied to people to work and they will have more income to save to buy any expensive medicines, if they are facing serious sickenss, e.g. cancer. Then, they can buy this cancer medicines to eat to treat cancer disease (non common sickness) in order to be more healthier.

Thus, economic growth can lead medical industry has enough money to carry on researching any new kinds of medicines to attempt to treat any serious diseases in order to provide different kinds of new medicines to human to eat to treat any serious diseases more healthier. For example, U.S., U.K. these both developed countries can remain long term good economic groth. So, these both countries have enough money to assist domestic hospitals to carry on researching any new kinds of medicines to let patients to choose the most effective or more healthier medicines to let patients eat to attempt to treat their serious diseases more successfully. So, U.S., U.K. serious diseases of patients whose death ratio is decreasing in these two countries as well as their death ratio, due to serious diseases causing is the least to compare to other countries.

Secondly, I shall indicate on the improvement in health and economic growth hand, how any why it has relationship between improvement of human health and economic health. I shall focuse in particular on the question of how much of the improvement in health can be attributed. The improvements in the health can include that human's living of standard, better nutrition, changes in the public health environment, it includes sanitation and supply of clean water. Finally an improvement in medical technology, for example, both sanitation improvements and treatment with antibiotics will reduce mortality from infectious diseases.

However, we can explain why economic growth and improvements of human's health , which has relationship. It can be measured by mortality, it can be linked to specific changes in both ages at which people, i.e. an increase age of the number of patients to disease, such as U.S. , U.K. these both countries, the number of old age people who have serious diseases of the total population ratio is less than the developing countries, e.g. China, Africa. It is possible to explain because these both countries have stable long term better economic growth to compare these both developing countries.

Thirdly, I shall indicate on the better nutrition of food supply and economic growth relationship hand. It seems that better economic growth in the country , it will encourage the country people have more consumption effort, then they have enough food to earn more better nutrition to live. So, their diseases will be reduced, due to they have enough food to supply to them to eat to earn more nutrition from different kinds of foods every day, e.g. beef, pork meat, vegetable , fruit etc. food. Hence, economic growth can encourage any food consumers have effort to spend too much expenditure to buy any kinds of fresh and good taste and better nutrition of food to eat. So, it implies the long term stable economic growth will encourage human to buy any kinds of better nutriction of food to eat every day. It can lead human has better healthier, due to human can hace more money to buy better nutriction of food to eat. It includes the special poor people who have effort to buy better nutriction of food to eat.

To sum up, the better nutrition of food is mainly to be consumed by the more effort of the country' poor people when the country have good economic growth environment. So, economic growth can lead any countries' hospitals to research more different kinds of medicines to be attempted to provide to any serious diseases patients to eat. The country's poor people can be raised more healthier to live in the stable economic growth countries.

● Sport industry development brings economic growth

I believe that economic growth must have relationship to influence human development. But it must not lead positive human development. Otherwise, when one country is experiencing stable economic growth in long term. It is possible to lead negative human development. I shall indicate as below:

To explain whether economy growth can influence human development. We need to research whether economy growth has relationship to influence human development. What is economic growth meaning? Economists explain it means an increase in gross national product (GNP) if all products and services that an economy produces during a specified time period. So, it brings one interesting question concerns economic growth: IS it a quantity based concept, not quality based concept? If economic growth is an only relationship to economic development Otherwise, if it also has quality based concepts, then it has relationship to influence or lead human development. When economy growth is a direct measure of changes in the size of the economy. Whether it is a measure of welfare to human development or sustainable development.

Why do we need to concern economic growth? Because political importance means domestic and international trading income and the country's people earning income measurement as well as humanitarian importance means an indicator of welfare, an indicator of human development and an indicator of sustainable development measurement. However, if seems GNP or GDP measures that value of products and services produces within an economy (economic income) in a given year, but it can also measure of welfare development, sustainable anything. Otherwise, human development includes welfare, which measures quality of life and human development, which means quality based concept as well as sustainable income, which means how much we can spend without running down capital stocks, we can maintain same level of spending in perpetuity. Hence, human development concerns our quality of life or standard of living. So, human welfare separation of means from a direct measure of well-being as well as economic welfare separation of means GNP or GDP corrected for expenditures on various necessities. So, it brings this question: Can GDP (economic growth measurement) be an indicator of human development or human welfare? I shall indicate cases to attempt to explain as below:

For GDP per capita and happiness case example, I assume that the country , US increases rapidly up to capita US $4,000 per capita in this year and small returns after that. What does this mean? What influences US people feel happy or happiness feeling causes? For another changing in GDP correlate to changes in environment quality case. Environmental KC (Kuznets Curve) showed the graphical representation of Kuznets theory from the 1940 year that economic inequality increases over time, then at a critical point begins to decrease. Environmental KC (EKC) shows a hypothesized relationship between various indicators of environmental degradation and income per capita.

The EKC (environment Kuznets Curve), shows that in the early stages of economic growth degradation and pollution increase, when beyond some level of income per capita , which varies for different indicators. The trend reverses , so that at high-income levels economic growth leads to environment improvement. This implies that the environment impact is an inverted u-sharped function of income per capita. Thus, EKC implies that economic growth has relationship to influence or lead environmental pollution causing, due to many factories are manufacturing any products during economic growth period. All air or water pollution will increase, due to factories manufacturers manufacture lot of products. The scale effort brings that economic growth increases environmental pollution if there is no change in other factors. The other factors include that change in output mix, change in input mix, state of technology, production efficiency and demand for " improved environment". Hence, when these factors have no change and factories need to use many resources to manufacture lot of products in the manufacturing process. It will bring serious pollution, due to these factories have not improved its technology, production efficiency to avoid to pollute environment to cause local pollutants, deforestation, biodiversity, river low quality, carbon and air low quality, waste increases with increased income. Hence, it is an evidence to explain economic growth will have possible to cause pollution indirectly as well as poor quality of life (standard of living) to influence our life. IT is a good evidence to explain how economic growth can lead human's quality of life (standard of living) to be poor. SO, it brings these questions as below:

Should we always aim to increase GDP? Should we choose to either gain ultimate happiness or either increasing GDP? Is it an indicator of wealth to depend on what GDP really measures? Should we need to concern environment degradation cost or our nervous stress from environmental pollution causing?

In conclusion, it implies that economic growth can lead positive human development , such as economic welfare influence, but it can also lead negative human welfare of long term air or water pollution influence and this challenge can not be solved to any countries in our life if any countries do not attempt to keep balance between achieving economic growth and clean environment in order to not influence our quality of life to be poor. The important evidence , it explain it has relationship between economic growth and human development and they have cause and effect relationship.

● Economic growth leads human employment growth

I believe that when one developed cuntry is experiencing stable economic growth, it can lead human employment growth in high technologic job market, but it can also bring unemployment to low knowledge or skill job, such as cleaning, laboring job market, due to artificial intelligence technology will replace many low skillful job in the future. I shall explain as below:

I assume that it has positive relationship between the accumulation of human capital relation to total employment and GDP growth. It means that a positive relationship between economic growth and the demand for qualified labor are consistent with the hypotheses of the form in the industrial export sector positively influenced by the accumulation of human capital. I shall explain the reason why economic growth can lead positive human employment growth as below:

Namik, (1965) explained that economic growth theories reflect on the continuous increases in the gross national product, because of interaction that occurs in a given environment; in a certain time period, including various changes in the presentation of productive factors in society labor, capital and nature resources to lead these radical changes to increase successive demand on commodities and hence an increase in national income.

Hence, society labor knowledge or skillful development will be one important factor to influence any country's economic growth. If the country has many good educational and skillful labor, then the country will have more possible to raise economic growth for long term, due to they can apply their expertise skills and knowledge to attribute to their country's different kinds of high skillful or knowledge jobs or occupations to do in order to raise themselves country's productivities efficiently. Hence, economic growth has more effort to raise human (labor) these knowledge or skillful development in possible. Considering how economic growth leads labor's skillful and knowledge development positively, I shall indicate these factors as below:

Firstly, on manufacturing industry labors development factor hand, I assume that China's industrial export sector has been positively influenced by the accumulation of human capital , due to many China young people who had graduated any different kinds of degrees, e.g. engineering, education, law, accounting, business, management, chemical , medical , architectural , biology, medicine, computer science, earth science, space science, ocean science, environmental science etc. different kinds of subjects from overseas universities or local universities. Them they apply their expertise knowledge to attribute their skills to do any kinds of professional jobs in China's society. Due to China's sudden economic growth , so it reflects on the continuous increase in the good gross national product, because it occurs in a given good economic environment in a certain time period, due to the global different kinds of China's product number need is increasing as well as many China product manufacturers need many high educational and skillful labors to attribute their effort to help them to develop their businesses in China during the good economic growth period. Hence, China's economic growth leads China's any kinds of product manufacturers who need to employ any kinds of high educational and skillful employees (labors) to do their different kinds of jobs , due to global any kinds of China product consumers' needs are increasing suddenly. Then, it causes the effort to China employees who prefer to spend expenditure to train any young graduated people to be qualified high educational skillful labors with the good conditions of production; which leads to competitive sectors to attract these lacking working experiences of young graduated people t to be the availability of qualified labors in China in order to raise enough employment supply number to satisfy China's manufacturers' labor needs. So, it is a reason to explain that China's high educational and skillful labors development aims to attract foreign investment at a time. The overseas countries seek to provide investment environment through international laws and regulated that only provide qualified labor able to deal with modern technology to China's manufacturing industry development. So, China's economic growth will lead China's knowledge and skillful labors development in possible.

Secondly, on human capital education accumulation factor hand, economic growth will lead human capital educational level to be raised. I shall explain that why economic growth can lead human capital education accumulation positive reason as below:

I shall suppose that the negative impacts in the economic growth rate, it will bring the poor qualified human capital education level. I believe that it has direct relationship between education and the economic growth rate. I shall also suppose that the principle variable of interest determining GDP per capita is the level of labor supply which accounts for all the different educational level, (i.e. primary education, secondary education and university education).

Human capital accumulation can be explained to contribute to utility maximization. In general, it is a direct contribution in the utility function, this is because the more human capital each individual can accumulate in terms of knowledge and skills, the more happiness will be obtained for each one. Hence, it brings this question: Why can economic growth lead human capital accumulation educational level to be raised? The reason is because that when one country has good economic growth, then any primary, secondary and university schools have enough effort or resource to raise teacher individual teaching skills in order to teach many high knowledge and skillful level of students and satisfy their learning needs. Hence, the factors of these primary, secondary and university schools' educational inputs will also be raised, such as the teacher individual characteristics, their educational quality and educational experiences and qualities of their educational services provided and the interest of the country in accumulating educational high level of human capital need. For example, when the country encounters a high economic growth rate, it is able to demand new technology ,as a result of its well-educated society , such as China is one developing country, it needs a well-educated society to educate or train its high educational or skillful labors when it is experiencing in one good economic growth period. So, China's firms encouraged to adopt the advanced technologies developed in high income countries , when global economic growth is coming. It will cause the country, such as China will need to educate many high educational and skillful level labors to do any kinds of high technological jobs in itself country. So, China is a developing country because it needs to develop high technological manufacturing industry, it explains how its economic growth leads high educational and skillful labors development.

Consequently, such as these two cases indicate that one country's economic growth will be possible to lead high educational and skillful labors development in order to raise its competitive ability in different kinds of industries. In specially, high technological development industry , it needs significant high number of educational and skillful labors to satisfy the country's labor market when it is experiencing good economic growth period because many country's high technological product industry is their main income source. So, when the these countries are experiencing good economic growth period, it will lead the human employment growth positive effect for this kind of industry in possible.

- Economic growth leads income inequality

I believe that when one country is experiencing stable economic growth, it will bring serious negative influence to raise income inequality bewteen high education and low education people's income. I shall explain the reasons as below:

Why does the country's economic growth lead negative income inequality influence? Does either the country's high economic growth lead high income inequality or its low economic growth lead low income inequality in appropriate rate? I shall explain that what reasons to lead income inequality, when the country has high or low economic growth influence as below:

Many economists believed that the relationship of reverse causation from inequality to growth. It has a negative relationship between high economic growth and income inequality. I assume that the gross domestic products per capita to the level of inequality in income distribution. The unequal distribution of income seems similarity to the economic development process.

In fact, the first time , the economic development tends to increase inequality, but the trend is reversed, inequality stabilizes, the decrease until it reaches the lowest level that can be seen in the industrialized economies. So, when the country is encountering farming or agricultural economies or this farming industry won't be easier to lead income inequality. Such as Africa is a farming industry African income level won't have significant income inequality, due to it lacks high technological economic development in itself country and its main jobs are most relate to farming, low technological and low educational need of different kinds of farming jobs. So, the high income and low income people's salaries are not significant difference too much. Otherwise, industrialized economic country, such as China, many Chinese workers are working in different kinds of industrialized jobs in China. However, although, the industrial industry brings economic growth in China society. But, China's high and low income of industrialized workers' wages, they have large significant difference. For example, the computer programmers and computer inventor salaries and the computer manufacturing workers' salaries, they have large significant difference, for another example, the vehicle designer and vehicle inventor salaries and vehicle manufacturing workers' salaries, they have large significant difference. Due to computer programmer or computer inventor needs have high technical knowledge, but computer manufacturing needs have low technical knowledge as well as vehicle designer or vehicle inventor needs have high vehicle components knowledge to invent any kinds of new styles of vehicles, so their salaries must have high income significant difference to compare the vehicle or computer manufacturing worker. Hence, due to their educational and skillful level is significant difference, so it causes their income will have much significant difference in industrialized industry.

Hence, although China is encountering economic growth, but it also leads high income inequality to China's labors, due to it is one industrialized country. For Africa farming country example, its main industry is agricultural sector, designed as the traditional low-productivity sector in the Africa economy and it can not be replaced easily by the industrial sector. In this traditional farming industry, Africa can not develop its economy to grow up easily. So, it leads its labors' salaries level , which has less or low income inequality causes. Otherwise, such as China is a industrialized industry country, it has different kinds of industrialized development of this sector, such as the computer manufacturing or computer program sector and the vehicle manufacturing and vehicle design invention sector, which produces a movement of labor form low-productivity to high productivity sector, e.g. the vehicle sector is one low number productivity sector and computer sector is one high number productivity sector. This is reflected by an increase in income inequality in China's industrialized society.

Hence, such as above cases, Africa is one farming country, so it causes economic growth is slow and African income level is less inequality. Otherwise, China is one industrialized country, so it causes economic growth is fact and Chinese's income level is more inequality. It can conclude that fast economic growth country will lead high income inequality. Otherwise, slow economic growth country will lead low income inequality. Banerjee and Newman (1993) indicated a relationship between the choice of occupation and the development process with the presence of an imperfect credit market. In this context, the occupation requiring a high level of investment is undoubtedly devoted to the wealthiest of the population. So, they believed that and industrialized countries will have more occupation choice to let themselves country's people to choose the best salary level of jobs to work. Due to industrialized development causes their economic growth is fact. So, it causes many occupations are created to let themselves country's workers to choose to work, then fast economic growth causes many occupations creating and it leads high income inequality. Otherwise , the farming countries, they have slow economic growth. So, it causes less occupations choice to let themselves people to choose to work and the slow economic growth countries will lead low income inequality.

Consequently, it explains that it has relationship between whether the country is industrialized economy or farming economy or technological economy as well as high economic growth or low economic growth . Then, it has also relationship between high or low economic growth and more or less occupation choices. In final, it has relationship between more or less occupation choices and high and low income inequality. In sum up, high or low economic growth will lead high or low income inequality in possible.

Reference

Iwasaki, Y., & Havitz, M.E. (1998). A path analytic model of the relationship between involvement, psychological commitment and loyalty. Journal of Leisure Research, 19(2), 256-280.

Zaichkowsky, J.L. (1985). Measuring the involvement construct. Journal of Consumer Research, 12(3), 341-352.

CHAPTER II

Tourism and the entertainment age:thought on an international travel phenomenon

Nowadays, tourism entertainment activity is very popular. Every country government must have itself tourism development strategy to seek how to persuade other countries' tourists choose to travel to its country in preference. So, tourism entertainment incomce will be one imporant market share to any countries' overall GDP income. How to excite other countries tourists to choose itself country to travel in preference. It is one interesting question to any countries' tourism policy decision market. I shall indicate some cases concern how to predict and excite travellers' entertainment psychology in order to bring attractive tourism experience to any countries as below:

THE USE OF SOCIAL MEDIA AND ITS IMPACTS ON TRAVELLER BEHAVIOUR

Nowadays, internet is popular to use. Social media enjoy a phenomenal success in terms of adoption and usage levels. They cause every day lives on how people connect and communicate with each other, on how they express and share ideas, and even on how they engage with products, brands, and organizations.Moreover, social media became significant networks of consumer knowledge. In travel and tourism, the impacts of social media have already been described as tremendous, primarily due to the experiential nature of tourism products, and especially of holiday trips: purchases are considered risky and therefore decision making processes are information intensive.

Moreover, social media is all about facilitating people to express and share ideas, thoughts, and opinions with others. It is also about enabling people to connect with others, like they were doing for the last thousands of years. However, what is of significance is that social media: (a) removed spatial and time constrains that were inherent in traditional methods of communications; (b) provided online tools that enable one to many sharing of multimedia content; and (c) employ easy to use interfaces that enable even non-specialists to share and connect. So, any travellers plan to go to anywhere to travel, they will apply internet to attempt to seek any countries' hotel price, air ticket price data as well as seek any countries' destination whether it has anywhere places or locations, they are worth to visit before they decide to go to the country to travel, even they will seek whether the country anywhere have any restaurants to provide the good taste food to them to eat, choosing which kinds of public transportation tools are the most cheapest or the fastest to arrive the destination to travel.

The travellers they will feel to make the accurate expenditure budget before they decide to go to the country to travel when they apply internet to seek any travelling data. Even , some travellers will apply internet media to discuss to other travellers by email media communication channel conveniently.

For example, facebook is the most popular social media

networing. During the last years social media are enjoying a phenomenal success: Facebook, a social networking website, many travellers like apply this facebook social media channel to discuss and share their travelling experience together. So, any travellers can apply faccebook social media to know whether

the country's any destinations , anywhere are worth to visit or not. Hence, if one traveller had planned to choose the country's some places to travel, but when he feel negative emotion when he discuss with another

traveller concerns his past travelling experience to his travelling planning destinaton. Then, he will be influenced to change another country's travelling destination to travel. Hence, facebook media brings the sudden and rapid travelling plan change to every travellers when they discuss their travelling experience

in their online travelling discuss process.Thus, online social media can bring these several aspects of influences to any gathering data online travellers. They may include as below:

It is one kind social media use and impact during the entire holiday travel process as well as throughout the holiday travel related consumer decision making processes. It influences during which stages of the holiday travel process to any travellers feel that they need to gather any travelling data from social media before they decide to travel any destination in habit. Hence, online social media can bring impact active users' travel related consumer behaviour in popular.

According to The World Wide Web Consortium (W3C 2004), the web has numerous impacts in society and culture, science, industry and business: In society and culture the web provides a new medium of worldwide human communication and revolutionized access to information and knowledge with implications in all aspects of the daily life from religion and sex to health, politics and commerce. In science, the web has drastically changed the way scientists are doing research: It enables real time access to an enormous amount of information via sophisticated but user-friendly search tools, facilitates cooperation between scientific communities, serves as a new platform for conducting primary research but also as a channel for the dissemination of scientific knowledge. Due to the web, consumer preferences and the decision making process are not influenced only by the traditionally defined controllable and uncontrollable stimuli. They are also influenced by the "web experience", or the "online atmospherics" consisting of online controllable factors such as website usability, interactivity, trust, aesthetics, online marketing mix (Constantinides 2004), and by the website's quality, interface, satisfaction and experience (Darley et al. 2010).

On the other hand, there are also signs of negative implications: The Internet and the web makes consumers highly individualistic, more time driven and demanding, more information intensive,dictating timing and mode of communication, and with increased expectations (Akehurst 2009).

In addition, the vast amount of information available on the web causes an information overload, impacting negatively on the ability of users to locate information relevant to their needs (Radosevich 1997). Thus, it seems that word wide web or internet invention which can influence travellers feel negative emotion very easy when they apply facebook social media to discuss themselves past travelling experiences. If some travellers often share their negative
travelling experiences to other from facebook social media, when the other travellers read their negative travelling feeling from the words and they will write down on paper to remember the travelling destinations are not value to attempt to travel.

Then, there are many travelling places are not very attractive to let many travellers to feel when they often share their negative travelling experiences from facebook social media. Although, some travellers want to find the best or the high value of travelling destinations to travel, they shall attempt to discuss or enquire any travellers' opinions from facebook social media. But, in fact, there are many travellers want to find the worst or the less value of travelling destinations from facebook discussion. Hence, facebook social media can influence many travellers' to change their prior destination choices to another later desitnation choices often, when they get the negative travelling experience to share together from the social media internet channel any time.

- Tourism industry element

The tourism industry relies a lot on services and operations; we can classify the operating sector into different hospitality, they may include: accommodation sector, trade trade sector,event sector,attractive sector,entertainment sector, adventure and recreation sector,tourism, transport sector and food sector. Each of the sectors above is different in the services it renders, but sometimes they rely on each other to be more efficient.

The entertainment sector which is the main focus of the research could also be categorized into different segments.These any one service sepect must be important elements to influence overall tourism income and they have close relationship. For example, when one traveller feel the hotel can provide comfortable feeling to satisfy their lving need in his short trip time as well as he can find any entertainment activities easily as well as he can find any cheap and fast public transportation to catch in his trip any time as well as he can find any restaurants to eat good taste food in his whole travelling trip when he visits this country first time. Then, all of these enjoyment and comfortable of travelling feeling will influence he remember this country is one valuable travelling place and he also feels that he ought continue to choose this country to travel again and again. So, if the country can provide the overall travelling activities to satisfy any traveller individual living, eating, transporting and entertainment need. Then, its tourism industry will develop rapidly. For example, theme Parks aims to create an atmosphere of another place and time, and usually concentrates on one dominant theme, around which architecture, landscaping, costumed personnel who are sometimes known as animators, and different facilities for entertainment, distraction, recreation, or physical activities, such as rides, shows, food service and merchandise, are coordinate, because the different facilities in a theme park belong to the same enterprise. (Weiermair,& Mathies, 2007, 228.) Examples are the Walt Disney Magic Kingdom, Disneyland, Sea World Florida, Europe Park Universal Studios and many more. Theme parks are majorly child-friendly, which makes them interesting places for families to visit and they are usually filled with numerous exciting rides, a carnival atmosphere, and several cartoon and movie characters.

On conclusion if any country hopes to develop itself tourism entertainment industry in success , one country needs to consider many different aspects of entertainment facilities to let travellers to feel fun, excite and comfortable and enjoyable in order to let them can not forget this travelling entertainment activity choice in his/her live. Because any travelling related service elements will have important influence to every first time traveller individual psychology, if the country's any travelling related services can provide the positive emotion to let every traveller to feel. Then, the repeating travellers number will have more chance to increase because they still feel this country can provide the best travelling entertainment service to let them to feel to compare other countries in their life.

- Traveling entertainment industry leads urban environmental planning development need

I beleive that when one country is experiencing stable economic growth, it must lead urban environmental planning development need, I shall indicate reasons as beow:

Can one country's long term stable economic growth lead urban environmental planning development to itself country? Do they have direct or indirect cause and effect relationship between them? I shall indicate some causes to explain whether they have cause and effect relationship between of them existed.

Mexico city is one good example to explain whether itself economic growth has relationship to lead itseld urban environmental planning development recently. Nowadays, Mexico city's economic growth is stable, so it has effort to develop a more livable interlinkage of economic social, and good environmental city to provide to Mexico people to live. It has been developing more livable city by building an efficient intra-urban bus system, expanding urban green space, and meeting the basic needs of the urban poor. Hence, it implies that when one country has long term stable economic growth effort, it is possible that it will plan to develop it's urban environment in order to let its people to live more comfortable, such as Mexico city recent urban environmental planning development core example. So, it explain that why economic growth will bring human's living needs to gain satisfaction in possible.

However, I bring one question: Does it has possible to develop the urban environmental development to achieve the most effective and beneficial to the country's cities , when it had been experiencing the long term stable economic growth period? I shall indiate some evidences to explain this issue whether it can be possible to occur as below:

Every country has thousands of possible sustainable cities, for each city has unique historical , cultural, political and environmental circumstances. Such as U.S. , U.K. these both countries, which have many cities, e.g. Washington, New York, London etc. cities. Every city has unique cultural, historical , political and environmental circumstances backgrounds. So, their urban environmental planning needed to be adapt from approaches formulated in cities and regions, where problems of infrastructure, social equity, and urbanization of the environment have been creatively addresses. They need to know how to design every city's urban to impact on the environment more adapt to make cities more livable for human.

In fact, in economic view point, due to our earth has limited natural resources will continue to provide life support for humanity's lives. So, every country needs to know how to use our earth's limited natural to use our earth's limited natural resources to develop every city's urban environment to let every city's people to live more comfortable to avoid the lacking enough earth's natural resources to be supplied to them to design urban environmental function for every city use in the future one day. Because every country's cities; human population tends to grow, but every country's cities' lands area supply is limited. So, it will cause every city's natural resource is not enough to supply to human to use, when the city's human population growing number has exceeded the city' land area supply to suppot the city's human normal population to live. Hence, it is a value considering question: How to use our earth's natural resource effectively and efficiently and organizing, e.g. land area. It can avoid future natural resource, such as land supply shortage causes human can not satisfy comfortable living environmental need in every cities.

Traditionally, economists have been concerned with the efficiency of resource use. They have been slow in developing economic models that adequately account for resource scarcity and pollution. Only rarely have economists worried that some resources may be short supply, such as clean land and soil , clean water, clear air and theat if these resources are used indiscriminately, they may become exhausted for every city population growth need for which, the city's urban environmental is needed to plan and develop. So, human expected to have comfortable lifestyles.

We need to know how to choose to do our behaviors to avoid environmental pollution, e.g. land, air, water qualities dirty pollution, when the country has long term stable economic growth, it can not neglect how to avoid environmental pollution to every city as the same time. So, when one country has long term stable economic growth. It also needs to plan how to reduce land, air, water natural resources are used by human's wrong attitudes or behaviors to use our earth's natural resources. So, it implies that when one country has long term stable economic growth, it also needs to consider how to plan to develop its urban environment efficiently and effectively and organizing in order to satisfy every city's people's comfortable living needs.

Hence, I bring this question: How to keep stable economic growth and enough natural resources supply to urban environmental development to different countries' cities? I recommend that when every country government needs to encourage businessmen consider environment protection issue when they choose to do and kinds of businesses in themselves countries.

Keating, (1993) explained that how to utilize local materials and are energy-efficient, non-polluting and labor intensive as well as every country government needs to achieve action progress of energy conservation and renewable energy, such as wind, solar, hydro-electric renewable energy, and biomass. For transport policies that favor public, bicycle, and food transport over automobiles municipal development designed to reduce commuting and land use that contains urban sprawl and prevents it from encroaching upon agriculturall land and environmentally sensitive areas are enunciated.

To sum up, in human development history, our earth was relatively empt of human beings and our belongings are only include (man-made capital) and relatively full of other species and our habitats (natural capital). In ago human development history, because human had no any business economic activites. So, human does not need to expand much natural resources to do any business economic activities. Hence, human had enough natural resource to be supplied to use. Till to nowadays, years of economic growth have changed that basic owning enough natural resource supply pattern. As a result, the limiting factor on future encouraging growth has changes. If man-made and natural capital were good substitutes for one another, then natural capital could be totally replaced.

How the two are complementary or however , which means that the short supply of one imposes limits. I shall indicate fishing boats catching fishes to sale business example to explain the economic growth and natural resource shortage relationship issue. If one day, the country's ocean had enough fishing boats to catch fished to sell, but it has without enough population of fishes to be caught to let the fishing boats to catch to sell in the ocean. Once the number of fish sold at market was primarily limited by the number of boats that could be built and manned, not limited by the number of fish in the sea. This suitation is better, due to the natural resources of fishes supply number is enough in the sea. It is only the fish catching boats number is not built enough factor. This cas is similiar to urban environmental development to cities case. When the country had developed long term stable economic growth ,it needs to consider whether human's standard of living is raising up or falling down as the same time. Such as this fishing boats catching fishes business case. If human only consider whether the fishes catching number is increasing every day . But human neglect to consider that one ocean will be polluted and fished will be killed by pollutants. Then, the shortage of different kinds of good taste fishes number challange will cause. Although, human has enough woods or steels resources to build any kinds of fishing boats, but it can't solve fishes shortage challenge. Then, it will lead fishes supply number shortge and it can lead human's living of standard to b fallen down, due to human has no enough fishes to be supplied to eat because many fishes are killed by pollutants in sea. It is similiar to human's urban environmental planning development case. When, human only consider how to remain long term stable economic growth, e.g. building many houses in the limited land area cities, it will damage the city's land green plant and tree growth natural environment as well as the city product manufacturers neglect to avoid to pollute river, air and ocean in their factories manufacturing process. Then , in long term time, when our natural environment is polluted. Any cities will have only polluted dirty air to human to breathe and dirty water to provide to human to drink and any cities lack enough green and clean soil to grow trees and plants to let human to live comfortable in different cities. Then, human's standard of living or quality of life will be fallen down. So, human ought consider economic growth will lead natural resources number to be decreased as well as environmental pollution challenge causes, due to human's economic action lead this challenge causes.

Consequently, economic growth has possible to lead urban environment planning development needs, due to human had polluted our natural environment and consume the exceed number of natural resource to cause any vegetable and fish and food supply number to be reduced in long term stable economic growth period to every country's economic development. To avoid human needs to reorganize cities and urban environmental development need. Huaman must need to find solutions to avoid to cause serious pollution to our land, sea and river and air in our long term stable economic growth period.

In conclusion, when one country is experiencing stable economic growth , it can perform better economic development. But, it can not absolute perform better human development. Due to human only considers how to do any business behavior to damage our natural environment and misuse our natural resource. Otherwise, when one country is not experiencing stable economic growth, it is possible to lead human development. Due to it's economic development stage is not reach the maximum period. So, the country won't do business behavior to damage its natural environment and misuse natural resource to cause itself people's standard of living to be worse.

reference

Akehurst, G., 2009. User generated content: the use of blogs for tourism organisations and
tourism consumers. Service Business, 3 (1), 51-61.

Constantinides, E., 2004. Influencing the online consumer's behavior: The web experience.
Internet Research, 14 (2), 111-126.

Darley, W. K., Blankson, C. and Luethge, D. J., 2010. Toward an integrated framework for
online consumer behavior and decision making process: A review. Psychology &
Marketing, 27 (2), 94-116.

Radosevich, L., 1997. Fixing Web-site Usability. InfoWorld, 19 (50), 81-82.

Weierman K, Mathies C, 2007, The tourism and leisure industry, shaping the future, Binghamton, Haworth press

World Wide Web Consortium (W3C), 2004. W3C 10th Anniversary [online]. Cambridge, MA:
World Wide Web Consortium. Available from: http://www.w3.org/2004/Talks/w3c10-

Overview/ [Accessed 12 December 2009].

CHAPTER III

The reader's reading method choice psychology

It is one interesting question to predict and measure why the reader chooses the book to study or how his /her reading habit behavior or
reading attitude which can influence her/his reading interest or reading book choice in this book sale market. I shall indicate some factors why and how influences reader individual reading behavior or book choice as below:

- Fair Pricing of The eBook or paperBook Perception Factor

Internet can influence buyer choice,such as whether the reader either choose to buy the ebook or paperbook choice .People will pay for convenience, entertainment, art, education, enlightenment, fun, the ability to have something instantly and many will even
pay a little more for a product that is friendly to the environment. In reading industry, ebooks are all of that and they can be read again and again
without costing readers more. People love to be entertained. They love to be enlightened. They love convenience. They love instant gratification.
So why is it that publishers are fighting a pricing battle for ebooks? For example, Amazon wants to see ebooks at $9.99 or less, publishers are fined for allegedly trying to price fix ebooks and readers demand to know why they should have to pay the same for an ebook as they do a paper book.
With authors, publishers, booksellers and consumers all trying to be heard on this topic of ebook prices the question persists; how much should ebooks cost?

In the economic "supply and demand" view, what cost to readers and to the publishing industry? Reading the flurry of articles written about
the DOJ's charges of price-fixing, as a reader, I initially felt like I was being taken advantage of. I must be, because the DOJ is forcing publishers to pay back some of the money readers paid for books. So obviously readers were over-charged, right? Not necessarily. And I realize that the charges against the publishers are about the conspiracy and not a reflection of what the government thinks ebooks should cost.

Regardless of what it costs to create a book, if no one is willing to pay the price publishers are asking then one of two things will happen; either publishers will offer less books, taking less chances on new authors, or publishers will have to cut costs in other ways to lower pricing. Or, perhaps, publishing houses are no longer needed. So, ebook publishers can replace paperbook publishers more easily if ebook price can keep very low to compare any one paper book price. Of course, a lot of people are speculating to benefit from self-publishing or are struggling to be part of an industry that can't afford them.

When publishers cut costs in order to meet the demands of readers for less expensive books, then the publishers can't take chances on publishing books that are not a sure bet to make money, leaving many out of work authors to move to self-publishing, setting lower prices that publishers are then expected match, which causes them to make less money from epublish online sale channel.

What does this have to do with ebook pricing? A lot really, because it causes us to focus on the side effect of the problem instead of the problem itself.

The problem is that no one is addressing the psychology of fair pricing of ebooks from the point of view of the end consumer; the reader.

Self-published authors are setting their own prices, often starting at $1.99. There are a lot of valid reasons to do this. The author may be looking to gain new readers by selling their back list, their previously published books in which the rights to the book have reverted back to the author, which is a good idea,

or the author may just be looking to make money by selling high quantities of books. Some authors are new and keep the prices low knowing many readers are more likely to purchase a book from an author they are unfamiliar with if the price is low enough. But, big publishers and authors,who have been serially rejected by publishers over the last few years, and are happy to hear the message of antiquated publishers in New York frightened of the future and how those publishers will one day regret rejecting the author.He is also an influencer. Recall that his site did not display a button for books that cost more than $9.99.

On the other hand, readers see the $9.99-or-less message in many places on the internet. Amazon favors the $9.99 price even when it means they will take a loss selling at that price. They do that as a business strategy to put other booksellers at a disadvantage and in some cases to put them out of business. And though most everyone in the industry knows of this practice and what its intent is, the government chose to see publishers as price-fixing when Apple and several New York publishers got together to

discuss how to combat the effects of Amazon's pricing tactics and try to figure
out how to take back their right to publish books at the prices they feel is fair.

Hence paper book publishers will face competition from ebook publishers because their prices are often lower than their general prices when they are displayed on an book shops.
What is a fair price for an ebook? How is that determined? It is determined by a lot of factors.
How much does it cost to create the ebook? How much is a reader willing to pay?

The problem is that publishers have not done one aspect of their job correctly. Yes, publishers do a lot of great things and they do it very well, but the one thing they should have excelled at, the failed at, and they are now paying the price for it. They have done nothing to create a psychology of fair pricing within the reader that matches the price they want to get for a book.

Publishers should be working on campaigns that promote books in ways that people are made to understand that a price of $15 – $25 for an ebook is a fair price. They should promote books so that people don't second guess what a fair price is. Do publishers not recognize the issues readers have with ebook pricing? Are they so focused on Amazon that they don't see the needs of their customers? However, paper books still have its attraction ,such as they can be sold, such as second hand book, when the book original buyer does not want to read the book, then he can sell cheaper price more easily. Otherwise, ebook can not resell to anyone in success because they are only read from internet channel. So, if the paper book is more attractive on reading and its price is reasonable, then I believe that it can still attract many readers to choose to buy it to read from book shop because readers believe it can be sold more easily.

Some points to make about ebook prices compared to paper book prices- People tend to think that having an actual, physical book in their hands, one they can share, re-sell, put on their coffee table and mark on (yes people do mark in their books), are all reasons why they are paying a higher price for a book.

Those are all good reasons, too. We will infer, for the sake of this lengthy article, that people include "good story" and "known author" as part of their acceptance to paying more. The issue seems to be that people feel an ebook has less value because you can't do those things with it. That is simply not the case. In fact, it's not paper and harder to display on your coffee table and you can't re-sell it or even share it as easily as you can a physical book but you're paying for something of equal value in the trade-off. You don't have to cart around heavy books everywhere you go. You can have instant gratification because you can buy the book and start reading it immediately from the comfort of your own home.

It is friendly to the environment. It is convenient, given that many books are available across platforms including your computer, mobile device and/or tablet as well as in some kind of cloud system. So if you forget your ereader at home, but have your mobile phone, you can still read your book.

On conclusion, there are things a reader can do with a physical, paper book that cannot be done with an ebook. There are things a reader can do with an ebook that cannot be done with a paper book. The reader is paying for preference. They are paying for what they want, how they want it. Where does that de-value ebooks in the mind of readers? That is the big question, isn't it?

Because it is easy to access a book online readers sometimes think ease, less valuable. But that's not true at all.

Ebook reading will become one kind of reading habit from mobile or laptop when the reader leaves his home in any time. Most readers will pay extra for life to be made easier for them. That's why there's valet parking and beauty salons. Yes, we can do those things ourselves, but we pay a lot of money each year to have other people do those things for us. Why? Because it's easier on us. So, ebook reading can let readers go to anywhere to read from their mobile or laptop. It is one kind of attractive new technological reading or learning behavior nowadays.

On conclusion, ebook reading habit will be replaced to traditional paper book reading habit in possible. Perspective is hard to change, especially once someone takes the lead and begins to create expectations. It is up to the publishing industry as a whole to band together and change the perspective of the reader when it comes to ebook pricing.

Hence, if paper book publishers hope to win their ebook publishers, they need to charge the reasonable book market price, it can not rise highly to compare its similar ebook topic, because when one ebook reader discover one ebook price is very low to compare one paper book, they have similar contents and topic , then he will prefer buy the similar topic and content ebook to read as well as the paper book must need to design photo to attract readers' reading interest and price is more reasonable in the paper book sale market. When he read the paper book long time, he feel bore to read, then he believe that he can sell this paper book (seond hand book) to anyone in less discount price more easily. When this both factors can achieve that the paper book will also be sold to anyone more easily.

- Electronic Publishing industry brings knowledge-based economic society

I believe that when one country is experiencing stable economic growth, it can raise knowledge -based economic society, I shall indicate reasons as below:

I shall explain why and how economic growth can raise the country to become one knowledge-based economic society. Knowledge investment means that knowledge distribution is through formal and informal networks, which is essential to economic performance, knowledge -based economies which are directly based on the production, distribution and use of knowledge and information. Knowledge is increasingly being codified and transmitted through computer an communications networks in the information societ. For example, the developed countries, e.g. U.S., U.K. . They have long term stable economic growth for may years. So, they had been experiencing the knowledge-based economic developed social coutries. Their knowledge-based economic societies will provide them the enabling organizational change at the U.S., U.K. firm level to maximize the benefits to them in both manufacturing and service technology for producing sectors.

The effect of "knowledge"-based economy, which will led a fuller recognition of the role of knowledge and technology in economic growth (human technologial capital) growth to assist or encourage human development. For example, the exports of high technology industries had grown fastly for these knowledge of economic growth developed countries, e.g. Canada, U.S. , U.K. , Australia, Japan, New Zealand, Europe etc. developed countries.

Knowledge-based economic development can also lead more intangible investments in research and development, training of the labor force, computer software and technical expertise to those above countries. So, knowledge-based economic development can lead human's talent development to create new talent human's knowledge to different technological development aspects, e.g. internet invention, 3 D printer invention, advanced medical equipment invention, space boats, nuclear energy invention, prior speed railway transportation tool invention etc. technological products. So, any one of high technological products invention which must need have good economic growth to the country, then when the country has good economic growth condition,it will have effort to train or educate talent human to attribute to knowledge -based societies to encourage or give these chance to talent human or inventors to invent any kinds of high technological products for human to use. Hence, when one country can have effort to be developed to one knowledge-based economic developed country. Then, it can have possible to provide high technological resources to educate or train " talent" humans or scientific inventors to invent any new kinds of high technological products to provide to human to use. So, in the future, oue standard of living will be improved in possible, due to economic growth causes any kinds of high technological products to be invented to provide human to use.

However, I bring this question: Can economic growth bring knowledge-based economic society to lead talent human development really? I shall indicate reasons to explain whether they have relationship to lead talent human development as below:

When the country has good economic growth , employers need skilled labor number will increase in the highest demand. Although, the manufacturing sector is losing jobs, but employment is growing in high-technology, science-based sectors ranging from computers to pharmaceuticals, high knowledge-based jobs. These jobs are more highly skilled and pay higher wages than those in low technology sectors, e.g. textiles and food processing. Moreover, knowledge-based jobs in service sectors are also growing strongly. Indeed, non-production or knowledge-based job in service sectors engage in the output of physical products are the employees in most demand in a wide range of activities from computer technicians, through physical therapists to marketing specialists. The use of new technologies, which are the engine of long -term gains in productivity and employment. Generally improve the " skills base" of the labor force in both manufacturing and services. And it is largely balance of technology that employers now pay more for knowledge than for manual work. So, it seems that economic growth will have possible to cause knowledge-based economic society to any countries.

Then, I shall explain the question: Can knowledge-based economic society lead talent human development? In fact, it is not a new idea that knowledg plays an important role in the economy . Also economists are now developing new growth theories to explain the forces which drive long-term economic growth. In new growth theory, knowledge can raise the returns on invetment, which can contribute to the accumulation of knowledge. It is done by stimulating more efficient methods of production organization as well as new and improved products and services. Knowledge can also spill over from one firm or industry to another with new ideas used repeatedly at little extra cost. Such spillovers can ease the constraints placed on growth by scarcity of capital.

Hence, it seems knowledge-based economic society will encourage employers to train talent human to contribute their any new kinds of knowledge to do any kinds of new creating jobs. Moreover, knowledge-based economy can also encourage employers to create more different kinds of new knowledge jobs to lead talent human development.

The talent human development includes these complex-areas of knowledge in order to fulfil their jobs as below:

For example, practitioners of law and medicine belong to know-who , it refers to knowledge about " facts ". This knowledge is close to what is normally called information. Know-why refers to scientific knowledge of the principles and laws of nature. It means technological development and product and process advances in most industries, e.g. research laboratories and universities organizations. So, firms need to interact with these organizations either through recruiting scientifically -trained labor or directly through contracts and joint activities. Know-how refers to skills or the capability to do something. A new product or a personnel manger neede to select and train staff have to use their know-how.

One of the most important reasons for the formation of industrial networks is the need for firms to be able to share and combine elements of know-how. Finally, this is why know-who because increasingly important. Know-who involves information about who knows what and who knows how to do what. It is possible that any talent human expects he.she knows how to use whose knowledge efficiently. The know-who kind of knowledge is internal to the organization to a higher degree than any other kind of knowledges. It is significant in economics, skills are widely disposed because of a highly developed division of labor among organization and experts. For example, for a modern manager who must need to own this kind of knowledge to manage whose organization efficiently and effectively in order to achieve the most maximum beneficial to productivities and raising employee individual working performance.

In conclusion, it seems that it explains why the knowledge-based economic country's employers need to spend expenditure to train talent humans in order to raise their different aspects of knowledge development, when the country is experiencing " knowledge-based economic society".

CHAPTER IV

Software entertainment game consumer behavior

How information technologic game strategy influences game player entertainment psychology? How and why information technological game strategy can influence economic growth? I shall explain as below:
Nowadays, Macrosoft and Microcorp are the global information technological big companies. They own much market share in global information technological industry. Whether what factors influence they can still be global information technological products leaders. Why does computer software consumers still choose their products to compare other software products in preference? I suppose that Macrosoft and Microcorp, their hypothetical any software games have developed a clever new computer game that is certain to be very popular. Although Microcorp have the unique competitive advantage with its own software game engineers and compete against Macrosoft, but it can so it cheaper and better if it can hire any Macrosoft's software game engineers. So, in economic view, it needs to pay high salary (higher cost) to hire Macrosoft's engineers (labor), but Macrosoft's engineers can help Microcorp to invent any new kinds of software games to compete Macrosoft. Although, Microsorp needs to pay higher labor cost, but when it can raise its any software games' design and game playing methods to attract any game players. Then, these new and exciting software games can help it can bring many game entertainment players and then it can sell cheaper price to raise more attractive effort to win its competitor (Macrosoft). So, higher software game designing engineers (skill labor), their game designing effort will be the major factor to influence any one information technological companies in success. If one software designing company can employ one high software game designing effort profession to help it to design any kinds of attractive software games. Although, it may pay high salary (labor cost), but it have much chance to attract many software game buyers to compare that if it pays less salary to employ one poor game software designing profession. Because the poor software game designing profession may need to spend long time to

research how to design any kinds of attractive game software to excite game players' playing desires in this playing software game industry market. Long time research to the poor software game designer may be one none any reward to compensate to the software game designing firm when it needs to pay long time salary to employ him. Otherwise, if the software game designing firm can accept to pay higher salary to the higher software game designer, he will have higher chance to help it to design any more attractive software games to influence game players' playing game entertainment desires. So, any software game designing companies their game designers (labor) must be the major factor to influence their business succeeds or fails in this software game entertainment market.

On the employing method hand, Microcorp can choose to include in its contracts with its software engineers that from working for another Macrosoft software company for a certain period of time if they resign from Macrosoft. A move such as this is sometimes called a preeptive move. Its propose is to alter its rivals' payoffs in order to alter their employing strategies. Preemptive moves are usually costly (high slaary), and this one is no exception. In its employment contracts makes Macrosoft a less attractive to let its old game software engineers want to leave their current employer, such as Macrosoft. As a result, Macrosoft must pay its software game designing engineers above the going market salary if it hopes their employment contracts can be continue between Macrosoft and its software game engineers.

Should Macrosoft must need to decide how to react. It can choose to fight Microcorp by aggressively advertising its game, which is costly high, but gives it a larger market share in the game player entertainment market, when Macrosoft had any one profession game software engineer(s) leave(s) his company and he/they change(s) to the another Microcorp software game designing company to work, or it can forego the expense of an advertisement campaign and simply share the market 50/50 with its major competitor, Microcorp to be partners.

Their competition has close relationship to influence economic growth because it will have many game players number to be increase if they can cooperate to be partners in success when they can design any new kinds of software game products to satisfy software game players' entertainment feeling. Otherwise, if they can not be one good partners and they only consider their every business benefits and neglect themsclvcs businçss benefits. Then, their software playing games sale price can either to be reduced in order to attract any software game players when their software games can not be designed to have much new playing methods to attract many game players. Consequently, the GDP income to this software game entertainment market must reduce because any kinds of entertainment software games prices are reduced as well as the game players number is also decreasing. Due to they are the major software entertainment game suppliers in global. Any game players will only choose either Microcorp or Macrosoft to buy their any kinds of entertainment software game products to play majorly. So, their software game manufacturing and sale number must influence global GDP income increases or decreases in macro economy view. It implies that any countries technological software game industry's GDP income will depend on these both Microcorp and Macrosoft software game's cooperation relationship whether they have good or bad cooperation relationship. If their cooperation relationship is good, then they can manufacture high quality and attractive entertainment software games as well as raising sale price and exciting many game players' entertainment desires to achieve the increase to game players number aim more easily.

How to achieve their cooperation relationship more easier. I suppose that, in the software game entertainment industry, over its lifetime, the computer game will generate $500,000 in new income (income minus production cost) for all the firms producing it or its clones. Macrosoft must pay its software engineers an additional $100,000 to get them to agree to accept a contract containing an anticompetition clause. It costs Microcorp $100,000 to develop the software if it can hire Macrosoft's engineers and $200,000 otherwise. Aggressive advertising costs Macrosoft $70,000 and has the effect of giving it a 80% market share if it restricts its engineers' employment and a 72% market share if it does not. So, the fall in total market share is caused by the fact that without some of Macrosoft's advertisements. If however, Macrosoft passively acquiesces to Microcorp's entry and shares the market, then both firms can still achieve a 50% market share fairly. Hence, they must need to achieve 50/50 market share if they hope to achieve the cooperation relationship in success. Otherwise, they will not achieve cooperation relationship in success.

However, the spending advertisement factor will also their cooperation chance in success. For example, it would be more realistic to recast the Software Game as one in which Macrosoft chooses how much to spend on advertising with sales depending continuously on the amount spent. Other examples of continuous cooperation choices may include: the productive capacity of an electrical power plant; the salary to offer a prospective employee; or the insurance premium to charge a prospective policyholder. So, the amount to any of these expenditure factor will influence whether they will decide to cooperate to sell their software games products in global game entertainment market.

How and why Macrosoft and Microcorp's cooperation can influence global economic growth? It is significant that Macrosoft and Microcorp both technological software game designing companies are global the largest firms, they are doing international software game trade business to many countries and they have large market share in the software entertainment game sale market. Aside from trade based on technological gaps and software game product cycles, software game entertainment industry is dynamic in nature or game players' entertainment taste will change any time in completely static in nature. That is, given the nation's game players' playing taste and game entertainment factor, such as game playing designing technological method and game player individual playing game taste both. We proceeded to determine the nation's comparative advantage and the gains from the different kinds of entertainment software game designing supply factor and the game player individual game taste changing factor. So, any nation's software game players number will depend on these both factors to influence whether their number will either increase or decrease in the year in this global software game entertainment market. However, these factors can be changed by time, technology usually can improve any software game playing methods and game player individual playing taste will also change any time. As a result, the nation's comparative advantage also changes over time, such as when the nation has many game players lose their interest to buy any software games to play, then the nation ought not only consider how to develop its software entertainment game in the technological industry, it is right time to research any other new technological industries to develop if it still hopes its GDP income can rise in the technological industry overall aspect. Such as dynamic trade theory is still in its infancy. However, our comparative statics analysis can carry us a long way in analyzing the effect on international trade resulting from changes in factor technology, and tastes over time, such as entertainment software game case.

The growth of factors of production will also influence the software game entertainment industry development, through time, a nation's population usually grows and with its size of its labor force , such as China and India. Similarly, by utilizing part of its resources to produce capital equipment, e.g. India needs to utilize its technological resources, technological engineers and technological material can need to be used to manufacture either new software game products or computers. But, its technological resources will be shortage (both labor and technological material). So, many technological companies choose to apply more technological material and technological engineers to use much time and money to manufacture any new software game products. Then, these labor and material resources will be reduced to be spent time and material to manufacture any new computer products in the year. In this technological industry case, capital refers to all the man-made means of production, such as machinery, factories, communication and education and training of labor force, all of which greatly enhance the nation's ability to produce either computer products or software game products. So, the national will also continue to assume that it can experiencing economic growth is producing two commodities, such as software game and computer both kinds of technological products under the constant returns to scale. So, if India can not raise the rapid technical process to skill labor and supply technological material supplying number to satisfy to manufacture the enough software game and computer products to supply them to sell to any countries' playing game players and computer users every month. Then, its technological industry will lose many clients, due to it can not supply enough software games and computers number to sell to any countries.

Several empirical studies have indicated that most the increase in real per capita income in technological industrial nations is due to technical progress and much less to capital accumulation. However, the analysis of technical progress is much more complex than the analysis of factor growth because there are several definitions and types of technical progress, and they can take place at different rates in the production of either or both commodities, such as software game and computer.

Technical progress is usually classified into neutral, labor saving , or capital saving. All technical progress , regardless of its types reduces the amount of both labor and capital required to produce any given level of output. So, if India could have good technical progress to raise its technological labor skill and reducing the technological material to be used to manufacture the software games and computers. Then, it will have chance to keep the maximum manufacturing level number to software game and computer products as the same time.

On conclusion, it is only Macrosoft and Microcorp's cooperation relationship can influence their any kinds of entertainment game products' playing qualities and entertainment taste to let game players feel more fun and exciting beacase when these both big high technological entertainment game designers like to attempt to cooperate to manufacture their any new kinds of entertainment game products to let children or young people to play in order to satisfy their exciting and actual enjoyment entertainment feeling when they can feel to be the actual person to participate to any game image environment influentically. Because their cooperation relationship can improve their game paying qualities and raise entertainment enjoyment performance more easily than the their competive relationship in this entertainment game market.

Reference

Banerjee, A. Newman, A. (1993). Occupational choice and the process of development . Journal of political economy, 101 (2). 274-298.

Keating, M. (1993). The earth summit's agenda for change. Geneva: centre for our common future, viii, x, 12-13. 63-67.

Namik, S.D. (1965). The theories of economic growth, Cario: Knowledge House.

CHAPTER V

Online vs offline book shop different development trend

Nowadays, online book publishing is one kind of popular sale method to global publishing. For example, Amazon publish is as a business model with many potential advantages, relative to a physical operation. It held out the potential of lower book inventing and distribution costs and reduced overhead. Consumers could find the books, they were looking for more easily and a variety book topic choices could be offered for sale. It can accept and fulfill orders from almost any domestic location with equal ease. And most purchasers made on its site would be exempt from sales tax. One Amazon strategy hand, it would have to make its returns and redress processes transparent and reliable, and offer other ways for clients to learn, as much about the book possible before buying. Future online book market development trend, such as Amazon, Barnes & Noble etc. online book shops. How closely would their clients find book ordering, as a substitute for visiting book stores?

In fact, Amazon is global the largest ingle online booksellers and sells many other products. Otherwise, Barnes & Noble, have been market share diminish obviously. In the future, Noble & Barnes both will have their market share diminish continue obviously. There are also many fewer specialty re lowest. Hence, it seems online and offline both publishing methods will be competitive. It brings this questions: What is the trend between online book sale channel, its size relative to offline book sales channel, growth rate and the charcteristcs of reders who by online in the future? How book market's online channels are economically different , due to e-commerce's effects on online book market and supply fundamentals? How an online book sales channel might be expected to change equilibrium market outcomes?

I believe online book channel based sale activity varies considerably on these aspects: Sales in manufacturing printing cost, online sale services and online demand print book sale book topic choices. Such as author online advertising, change more or less sale price, online paper book shipping cost, visa card discount or online book shop member card discount book purchase, what welfares to online book buyers are.

Why readers choose to buy books from internet habit? In tradition, online book buyers habit hope to use the internet to buy. Generally, they have these characteristics: They hope to use the internet to buy electronic books at home, they enjoy to read electronic book from computer, it is in any regular capacity , not nceecessarily to visit book shops to find books to buy and they can search any electronic from internet, electronic book is convenient to read from computer or laptop when they catch transportation or going to anywhere. Usually, internet users are higher income, more educated and younger. It seems that education is a sizeable determinant of who is online, even controlling for income. However, gender does not seems to be a factor in explaining internet use. Moreover, many of book qualitative patterns are seen for online book purchases in general are observed for electronic book products on on demand printing book products in particular.

Predition in future, many of the traditional online products , such as electronic or print on demand books, computer hardware , electronic airline tickets, saw more modest , but still substantial growth. In the future, online sellers trend to be newer online book stores and have less brand or reputation capital to signal or famous brand quality. These factors can create in online book sellers, which also often involve delay. However, there are many reasons for online book purchasing. The most obvious is that readers don't have opportunity where unobservable inferior point of electronic or demand on print book purchases.

● Pricing strategy in online and offline
book retailing

The book price represents consumer behavior on price. On one hand, the model contains two probability fuctions which render consumers' reservation prices for each individual channel. On the other hand, it is based on numerous book distribution which represent probabilities from and to each online or offline book store separate channel. Price strategy of book sale concerns how readers select a particualr book? Both offine and online book information seeking price strategies point out the challenges for information systems development. Hence, book price decision based on readers' age, e.g. children book price will be chealer than adult book price, due to children book content is usually simple and papers page is less. Otherwise, adult book content is more complicated or difficult to understand and page number is more than children book page number. However, online book store disadvantages are that : information system still often fail in supporting the users in causal leisure situations. In order to improve online book search system. Online book stores need to be better understood user strategies and performance and translate them into purposeful features.

A common analysis approach is to compare price and user strategies and interactions in the digital environment with those that occue in similar physical environment. If online bookstores hope to decide more reasonable electronic books or on demand printing books sale prices to compete with offline bookstores. Since, the physical environment (in this particular case bookstores) usually preceds the development of digital environments, processes and strategies from interaction in the physical environment have already stabilized and experiences can be translated into patterns for digital information system development. Thus, some only digital electronic bookstores , such as Amazon publish' disadvantages are : It lacks physical bookstore environment sale experiences. Otherwise, some owning themselves physical book and online book sale environment bookstores, bookstores that can compare only either paper books or electronic books bookstores to predict what the reasonable sale book sale price more easily.

Are these differences between online/digital book discovery environments and offline (neighborhood bookstore) services? Are researching recommendation strategies differences between observable in online and offline book search sessions? In general, interactive users studies based on user interactions in a ISBS developed web-based book discovery information system are aggregated cross multiple researcher groups. In order to provide a realistic book discovery environment, book collection should be large and comparable to other book discovery systems ,such as online book sale. For example, Amazon library book collection is used consisting of approximately 1.5 million books. Each book contains general metadata (title, authors, publisher, publication , year, etc.) subject metadata (classification, code), subject headings , user generated content (Amazon publish user reviewer, library thing user tags).

- How does India book market trend?

Thus, I believe that online or offline bookstore different book research method will also influence readers' preferable book choices, then their choices behavior will influence how many times to find the book easily. If the online or offline readers can find the book topic or author name or contents etc. information easily. Then, the sale chance of the book will increase. Thus, price can increase more. For high population country, e.g. India, China . Does it have more sale chance, due to many people are living in these countries? What us online book store trend in India? Online book can let readers to buy new books and old books from internet, rent or borrow books from internet or access it in the form of e book, e.g. Amazon publish is the big player of online book business in India today. India where dynamic technologies like mobiles are prevalent, e-book readers may soon make into average household. Some of publishing houses which predicted that it would be long journey for e –books to become part of life needs to India readers. Thus, India will be one potential e book market. India is the third biggest market for English books. However, there are challenges of online bookstore in India. IN fact, online book market has changed the way reading consumer use internet for knowledge. Nowadays, people prefer e books are accessible anywhere, any time for creating flexible and secure online bookstore for online bookstores that need to concern to sell their e books to India markets because India readers shall concern visa card payment method where it is safe to pay to read any e books from internet.

Besides, online information searching has touched every field of human life. In the future, it is possible that purchased via mobile are clothing/ footwear and e book or on demand print books. Also , due to e book is one kind of popular reading product to be enter India market. Currently, the online book market in India is offering exciting and renewed services to the internet users. India readers can accept to buy old books to read from online sale channel. Thus, India will be one new second hand online book store market to follow developed countries, such as US, UK etc.

● Trend and development on the global book market

Under the influence of internet, new media , social networks. The way in which search to satisfy our needs. Internet is the high technological search method to change at the level of products and services, such as e book (electronic book or demand on print electronic paper book) and online e book rent service , online library e book borrowing services. Thus, in the future, global book market will be popular on concentrating selling e books or online print on demand paper books more than general walk in offline book shop paper books sale only method. Due to, internet changes traditional readers' reading habits to enjoy to read e books from mobiles, laptops, desktops more than paper book reading. Thus, the global book market will be predicted online electronic book sale format more than visiting walk in book ship sale format. The digitalization of information enables us to bring into discussion today contents separated from the physical, materials, paper shapes of the book. Today, books could be found online, read online for free or downloaded as an e book in English or any other language. Practically, the book has changed from paper to electronic book. In until , the internet and the e book , the changes were extremely slow. Today, digitalization produces rapid changes to the entire system of printing, distribution and reading books. Hence, the global book market trend will be the major implication on publishes, distribution, authors and book consumers. The online competition brings major changes to traditional distributors, the bookstores, the author of independent distributors noticeable decreased. The number of big distributors' stores will decrease. For example, Amazon publish is the best known global selling books online. Although, it can sell e books and printing on demand paper books both from internet channel conveniently.

In conclusion, e book market will dominate global online electronic book sale market and the e book publisher number will increase. As the same time, the visiting walk in offline book shop number will decrease, due to readers have accept to use laptops, mobiles to read electronic books from internet channel more than reading paper books. It implies paper book publishers need to change sale method, e.g. adopting internet to sell print on demand paper books, or reducing paper book sale price to attract e book readers to choose to buy paper books to read.

- Web vs School campus book store development trend

Why do students choose to buy textbooks online? What factors motivate students choose online textbooks purchase? Nowadays, many online book retailers, such as Varsity books.com and Bigword.com ,. Amazon publish.com are now capturing more of the textbook online store market. What is motivating this behavior changes to student market , instead of children story market, entertainment or travel or sport book market etc. topic market. What causes students to choose purchase textbooks online ? Can likelihood to make purchases online by predicted by various social and personal characteristics of consumers? The online textbook purchase growth is allowing online retailers to capture a substantial portion of sales in some sectors. What motivates consumers to shop on the web? But, what if these factors are nor significant , such as better product availability, lower cost, as is that case when comparing on offline textbook purchasing.

There is no significant price advantage to buy textbook online, it is there an availability issue, given that textbook can be purchased in the campus store (Foucault et al., 2000).

I shall assume that precious positive online purchase is positively correlated with the likelihood of an individual purchasing textbooks online. Hence, it influences why readers choose to buy textbooks online again. Following , other factor web consumers are likely shop online to save time and/or money, but what of those consumers who shop online when an equally time and cost efficient alternative is present. With regard to textbook purchasing, the time invested in researching for the appropriate books is likely to be similar, regardless of whether the student bookstore or through an online textbook. With regard to textbook purchasing, the time invested in researching from the time invested in searching appropriate books is likely to be similar: regardless of whether the student chooses to shop in the campus bookstore or through an online textbook retailer. If time from purchase until use counts, online textbook shopping could be considered less time efficient than its offline counterpart. Due to the readers need to turn on computer to link to internet to read electronic books or wait the print on demand to buy paper books from the electronic book store web site to wait the paper books to post to the online book buyer's home. Otherwise, offline bookstores can reduce time spending to wait the books to be posted to the buyer's home, after who pay money to take the paper book from the bookstore immediately. So, the non-waiting post book issue is still the text bookstore's strength to attract students to buy.

Prediction of direction of electronic books future trend

What is future trend of electronic book publishing development? To answer this question, we need to know what benefits of (electronic books) can attribute to human's needs. Nowadays, electronic books (e-books) are one way to enhance the digital library with global 24 hours a day and 7 days a week access to authoritative information, and there enable users to quickly retrieve and access specific research materials easily, quickly and effectively. Evenm some ebooks publishers choose to let readers who can borrow ebooks to online readers to read from online libraries to earn profit. For example, Amazon publisher lets every Amazon readers only pay about US$5 per month. Then, who can borrow unlimited ebooks to read from

Amazon publisher private online member library website convenently.

Thus, it is one ebooks online borrowing strategy to compette with offline book stores and public library and school library in publishing industry. Due to offline book stores lack borrowing books services to any walk in readers. However, some countries' publich libraries also have similar ebooks borrowing to read services. An an ebook providers' electonic online libraries, online computer library center has been involved in the selection, catalogue and distribution of ebooks. Library users can able to remotely search, locate and checkout ebooks from the library's online public access catalogues. Thus, ebook publisher will have another public library competitor which can provide similar ebook borrowing service to online ebook readers from public library websites.

It means ebook publishers need to adopt any attractive ebook library sale borrowing service strategy to attract public library readers. However, as with any new opportunity, new challenge utilizes the internet opportunity to deliver new book content is no exception, Integrating ebooks into the digital library has created challenges and opportunities for librarians, publishers and ebooks providers for librarians in this ebook library borrowing service market to earn extra ebook lending service income. Because, online borrowing service library can have ebooks borrowing service, then why online ebook readers need to choose independent ebook publisher individual borrowing book service website to replace traditional public library paper book borrowing service. The reasons possible include that the readers can borrow ebooks to study from ebook publisher individual library borrowing website at home conveniently, but it is possible that they can not find any paper books to borrow from public libraries which are the same ebooks to be borrowed from any one ebook store to read, also ebook publishers can let whose ebook borrowers to borrow unlimited ebooks to read and there are longer extend borrowing ebook return days more than public libraries borrowing book return days and ebook readers have no penalty when they return ebooks too late and they can choose to pay little borrowing ebook charge in the month, if who do not expect to borrow any ebooks in the month, who can choose to stop to pay borrowing ebook charge in the month. Hence, they can choose to continue to borrow unlimited ebook numbers from ebook publishers and they are permitted to return ebooks longer time to compare traditional public libraries. For example, when the ebook reader pay only US$5 ebook library service fee to the ebook publisher in the month , then who can borrow the number of ebook up to 50 maximum number in the month as well as who can return the all ebooks to the ebook library within 60 days, it is longer return days to compare traditional public libraries. If the ebook reader can not return all these ebooks after the return day of 60 day. They can permit to extend more 60 return days. After this another 60 return days, they only need to pay US$5 penalty to the ebook store. Thus, it is one attrative ebook library borrowing service strategy in this competitive book publishing industry.

There is no doubt that the same trends that adopts ebooks and e-readers to US ebook publishing market are having a similar effect in other countries as well, such as Mobile ebook or laptop ebook technical development of reading devices that provide an reading experience similar to that of reading an actual book, the increasing penetration of the internet in all areas of life, which is significantly changing reading patterns and reading behavior. The increasing extent to which ebook or demand on printing book consumers are open to new technological reading trends, for which in particular that availability of attractive mobile devices, such as smartphones, portable games consoles, and MPS players are responsible to ebook reader tools.

Future trend will be that publishers and authors need to build close digital cooperation relationship. Publishers, bookstores and device manufacturers should take the opportunity to provide the market now with innovative ebook publishing products. And authors should explore opportunities for digital distributions and support publishers in their efforts to publish content. Publishers should also design a giving strategy and attractive ebook sale website that attracts customers without undermining the value of content. A well-thought out pricing strategy may also help publishers and content gain new customers, those who would not have purchased a traditional book , but may be inclined to buy an ebook that costs less, offers additional features , and works on a digital device . They already own there, usually the ebook price compares to traditional paper book price which have similar content, ebook price will be cheaper them the similar content of traditional paper book sale price.

In the future, ebook publishers will need to position themselves as content providers, and not just the suppliers of physical books. They will have to make content available on multiples media, in multiple formats, on multiple platforms. This content may not be limited to the text of a book itself, it may also include videos and games. This additional content may lead to incremental revenue.

In fact, the only leisure activities more popular than reading books were watching television, listening to music such the radio and reading newspapers and magazines. Thus, every one should need to choose to enjoy to do what kinds of leisure activities every day. For example, if one person chooses to spend much time to either watch television or listen the music and radio or read newspapers and magazines in the whole day. I believe that he will spend less time to read book in the day. Then, it implies that ebook or paper book readers , the paper book or ebook buyer number will be decrease, due to they spend less time to read or without any reading behavior in the day. Thus, how to persuade every one to feel that reading book habit is attractive or important which can be one factor to influence the paper or electronic book readers, even electronic or paper book buyer number. Thus issue will be an attractive topic to concern for every ebook or paper book publisher on book publishing industry. If these both kind of publishers can persuade any person to feel reading book habit can bring benefits to themselves. They will spend less time to leisure activities. Then, ebook or paper book sale number or ebook borrowing service income will raise in the future. Thus, these both kinds of publishers need to concern how to persuade people to choose to spend some time to read books habitually every day. Consequently, psychological factor will be one important direction to raise book buyer number in publishing industry.

What are the factors to influence sales and marketing strategies for publishers?

I feel that how to predict book buyers which is driven by book buying experience and the publisher's credibility (loyalty) factors which will influence the any book buyer whose make final decision to buy the book from the publisher. As a publisher, a major goal is to extend whose readership and extend whose readers' influences, but where to start? How do publishers understand and serve diverse readers and decision makers in different countries? Whether can readers find the kind topic of book from publishers only, when find the kind topic of book from the university libraries or public libraries? Hence, due to offline and online publishing industry competition is high, global publishers will need to develop a sales plan to satisfy readers' reading taste. For publishers need to conduct book exhibition activities, visit different author's decision makers to research what who like to write negotiate terms to publish books with individual authors, secure sales and manage orders etc. different regulations of publishing to every author.

I recommend online or offline publisher ought concern how to publish every book before they decide to sel their every electronic book or paper book to any countries' readers. The marketing strategy includes to develop plan every book sale projection, SWOT (strengths, weaknesses, opportunities, or threats) to every book to be published to the country's readers to implement the plan. Book sales program, email communication marketing, lead generation to analyze the results, eg. every book purchasing trends, customer profiles, marketing sementation for every book to follow up and bedrief: Measuring ROI, setting priorities and develops tastics, finally customer needs analysis foe every book sale, it includes GAP analysis, ebook online library visits numbers to experience the ebook and focus groups. The, it is cycle to the develop plan again. Thus, if the publisher can have a better understanding of pricing strategy plan which can create price plan to be strengthed changes or cancelled for every paper book or electronic book sale marketing price strategies. Bringing potentially and disastrous reading experience to readers , this factor can be one good method to increase reader number and book sale price and sale number method. Then, the ebook or paper book publishers can make more accurate ebook or paper book sale price to every sale market, e.g. US or UK which is better book sale market, which kind of book can be the popular to these either market, whether UK readers like to read ebooks more or US readers like to read ebooks more or US readers like to read paper books more or UK readers like to read paper books more. Thus, the ebook or paper book stores can gather these data to analyze whether what every book topic sale price is more accurate to achieve the highest sale number and income.

Consequently, more appealing offerings can be developed to broader every publisher's audience and enhanced whose every publisher's image, segments of reader research, e.g. reader age, book reading taste. This is a measure level of penetration of journals and identity opportunity for growth GAP analysis marketing strategies will be popular methods to future book publishing. Based on first hand, expensive visiting and surveying librarians around the world, examine factors unique to each country and culture and make to recommendations integrate in every publisher's communication plan. For example, ebook trends percentage of ebook spending in online ebook borrowing libraries is a publishing extra income from ebook borrowing readers. It is such one part of the overall electronic book market share income in the electronic book publishing market. In conclusion, internet technological innovation can bring new publishing business chance to ebook development , but it also brings competition to traditional paper book stores. So, paper book stores need have good marketing strategies to win their new ebook competitors.

CHAPTER VI

The difference between online and offline travel agents

1.1 The main cost related factors to offline or online travel agents

Nowadays,many online or offline travel agents have interest to find what the main factors that can affect their strategies to reduce airline costs. The main factors include route structure, type and characteristics of the aircracft, cost of labor and management quality, which will influence whether which airline routes are the most suitable to let online travel agents or offline travel agents to help them to sell paper air tickets or electronic air tickets to attract travel consumption more easily.

Thus, a cost-related strategy is the main important factors to influence travel consumption choice between online or offline travel agents. For example, considering that advantages in costs is an important strategy for carriers to remain in travel transportation market.

The deregulation process of travel markets and increasing opportunities for competition have created excess capacity in many markets that causes lower rates, even with its rising costs. Thus, the travel strategic costs management as well as travel consumers that their behavior under different influences can bring competitive advantages over travel players.

Cost reduction in the travel market -based industry is a very important way of being competitive between offline and online travel agents, when facing travel air ticket prices decreasing for every trip. So reduce to total travel cost, e.g. fuel, maintenance, labor etc. is relevant, but the influence of each component on every total trip cost depends on factors that are related or not to airline operation. For example, some airline can adopt the lowest cost model to sell air tickets from offline or online travel agents which compete for travel passengers with traditional modes as self driving road transport trip in large areas of countries domestic travel market, such as US, UK domestic travel market.

However, the decision about the relevance of one cost is not a simple matter. The effectiveness of reduction of each item that comprises the total cost of airline can change over time, depending on both the business model and the scope of the airline company or online /offline travel agent company as well as external factors.

However, there are three types of competition advantage between online and offline travel market: They are such as agility, differentiation cost and the differentiation may be related to a product of superior quality, higher value f the brand or the company's positive reputation. Such as the online travel agent's providing the different airline cheap air ticket price and kind of trips to provide to travel consumer consumer comparison or the offline travel agent's famous brand or positive reputation to let travel consumers feel travel agents can provide many actual trip package to let them to compare by oral clearly. Thus, the online travel agent's weakness is lack of travel agent individual exploration to let every travel consumer to understand every trip package more clearly.

But online travel agent's strength is it can provdide one website to let travel consumer attempt to compare different trip air ticket and/or hotel price to make personal travel pre-booking decision at home. The another advantage is related to techniques that reduce production cost, making it is possible to offer cheaper air ticket, or hotel room rents, or cheap trip package, than the competition. Such as online travel agent can sell more cheape electronic air ticket price to compare traditional offline travel agent's paper air ticket price.

Finally, agility refers to the speed which the company responds to market demands. For example, if the online travel agent can make statistics to analyze how many online travel consumers to choose to buy which airlines' electronic or paper air tickets, e.g. which airline trip destinations and trips and hotels choices are the most popular attraction to them. Then, the online airline has possible to respond to provide to the most popular airline trips choices, electronic air ticket price comparison choices and hotel rooms prices choices to attract many online travel consumers to enter their online travel websites to choose different airline electronic tickets to buy or pre-book hotel rooms from travel agent websites. Also, if the traditional offline travel agents can attempt to gather every travel consumer's destination trips, hotels , airline paper or electronic ticket prices enquires to make statistics to make which travel trip journeys or destinations and airline paper travel ticket prices are the most popular. Then, it is possible that they can respond to every travel consumer individual demand more to attract whose travel agent choice more easily.

1.2 Airline travel agency AirAsia in the domestic airline low cost strategy

There are three major characteristics of the airline industry namely is product nature, its expenditure structure and its market entry conditions. Airline agent's product is homogeneous or undifferentiated , causing significant competition in airline domestic travel or foreign travel both markets, which are free from regulations and economic barriers. However, high capital and operating expenditure is another important characteristic of the airline industry. Aircrafts, airlines' major capital expenditure are very costly to acquire . For operating expenditures, aviation fuel and labor make up the two major costs in the industry.

Another important characteristic of the airline industry is the conditions for market entry, which differs between international and domestic airline markets . In the international travel market, airline travel agency entry is very difficult as international flights and routes are the results of regotiations between governments . On the other hand, in the domestic and regional travel market, travel agency entry depends on the level of deregulation or liberalisation.

More and more countries, however are opening up their domestic travel markets for more competition. In addition, government plays an important role to regulate the travel markets and existing players may significant influence over now travel agent entrants.

In fact, the mjor factors influence to international or domestic travel consumption increasing numbers are the global economy and safety issues, instead of other different economic factors, such as travel destination choice, electronic air ticket or paper air ticket price, hotel price , the country's political change, e.g. war occurrence, bad weather , e.g. very cold or very hot etc. different factors infuence. Because generally , the world or any region of it is in an economic crisis or depression , the demand for airline services will fall. The late 1990 year Asian financial crisis for example, resulted in minimal increase in the number of worldwide airline passengers incrased only minimally from 1997 to 1998 year. Another factor of influencing the travel passenger number to be decreased, it concerns safety issues are also an important driver of the travel industry, which is subject to very safety standards to influence travel passengers' travel choice to the country. In addition, they are also unexpected safety related events, such as the 11 Sept. 2001 year tragedy in the US, which caused reduction in passengers . The increasing popularity of low cost airlines is the newest trend in the airline industry if which hope many passengers choose to buy whose electronic air ticket or paper air ticket to catch which planes to fly from online travel agent or offline travel agent channels.

The rise of low cost airlines, such as AmericaWest, JetBlue and Airtran in US, Ryanair and EasyJet in Europe and Vigin Blue in Australia. The share of low cost airline strategy is popular in the US and European airline market. For example, the Southwest airline low cost strategy is the basis of most low cost airlines operations. The key of the strategy is to reduce costs when at the same time offering low prices to passengers. History showed that the low cost airline strategy is easy to replicate , but difficult to implement successfully.

However, I suggest airlines need to know what functions which can attract passengers to chose to catch their planes to fly if they expect to rise passenger numbers. For example, the critical function of the Malaysia airline travel is to connect the major towns and remote interior areas within East Malaysia, which has poor road systems and limited availability of other significant means of transportation . In contrast, West Malaysia has more developed and extensive rod and railway systems.

Therefore, airline travel is not the main mode of long distance transportation. It implies Malaysis airline ought concentrate on focusing short distance transportation strategy for passenger beneficial choice function. For example, a new small Malaysia airline serving one or two routes may enter easily. Otherwise, a larger airline servicing multiple routes may be harder to enter Malaysis airline market. It also means access to capital and labor are the major obstacles for new airline entrants to Malaysia airline market. Thus, small airlines into a larger airline is probably more likely to be successful as in Air Asia's case to Malaysia airline market.

Thus, the airline low cost strategy competition positions include very low or minimal pressive from other airline similar service substitute products, low or medium power of airline similar input suppliers. In conclusion, low cost airline strategy is a god method to be attempted to win competitors in airline market.

1.3 How consumers select travel service between online and offline mode in travel industry

Nowadays, the travel industry is operating through two different modes, online and offline respectively. It involves the identification of the competitive strategies adopted by the tour operators. For example, it was found that e-retil travel is platform that is bringing two market forced the demand and supply tour operators and the customers together, and both parties and more inclined towards online mode in near future. Tour operators are gaining by operating at low cost and increasing their business reach when customers get what they desire as per their convenience. For example, many tour operators had promoted tourism destination through website that allow user to use interface for booking transporttion, foreign exchange etc. However, the role of travel operators (agents) should be assisted any airlines to promote their travel package service by internet more easily , such as tourism destination , arrangement of hospitality, restaurants, transportation tools during their trips.

The reasons why consumers choose online travel service include:

Firstly, it is online researching hospitality service. Online travel websites can provide many different accommodation furniture, such as seeking hotel locations, rooms prices comparison, prepaid hotel rooms by visa card payment transaction method, range from luxury five stars deluxe category hotels to small guest houses. The primary need of tourist is to find a place for residing in foreign country or domestic country to ensure whose safety and relaxing needs. Online travel website channel can help whom to find a place , according to his/her needs and paying capacity in the most shorten times.

Secondly, it is online restaurant (food and beverages researching) service. Full service restaurants are divided into two categories, fine dining and casual dining restaurants . Fine dining restaurants are usually located in the premises of luxury hotels, provide high quality food at premium price with good ambience and highly trained professionals. Thus, travel consumers can also compare the different restaurant food price and seek where is the restaurant and find.

What food taste of food supply from the travel agency or travel operator website easily 250 + tour operators are registered with the ministry of tourism (website of tourism ministry) , and the major players in the industry are dealing online and are dominating the travel industry. The major online travel players are Thomas cook, Cox and Kings, make any trips, clear trip, gatra.com and Expedia.

The tour operators whether online or offline offers a large number of services to the tourists including customized package where the customer selects each element of the tour package, specialized tourism package and complete tour guide package.

Nowadays, the tour operational travel (agents) are working through two different modes: offline online . Big brands with luge investment are dealing online and enjoying low cost benefits and huge profit margins. When the small tour operators have their market niche and managing have their market niche and managing their profits by dealing offline.

It is generally prefer offline mode that is the opportunity for small capital investment or employee number for tour operators. But the large scenario is changing as with the usage of internet by the tour operations have given convenience to the customers and now the customers of modern age have started developing preference for online modern. Thus, internet technology change any countries' travel agents or tour operators' air ticket sale method. So, it brings electronic ticket sale method is more popular to compare to traditional travel paper air ticket sale method.

However, online electronic ticket sale method has its disadvantages such as online transaction is unsafe, if the consumer 's name and address and visa card number is stolen to let any internet users to know to be used to buy any products from internet channel easily. Otherwise, traditional walk in offline travel paper ticket sale method is more safe, because the travel consumers can pay cash to the travel agents directly.

However, offline travel agent disadvantages include that the research identified that information communication and technology has very crucial role for tourism industry. Tourist can access any kind of information about tourism destination and tourism products from any part of the world. Tourism comprehends with social media. For example, it was found that (ICT) is bosting up tourism industry. (ICT) helps in searching the location, search for information on tourism products, and e-booking of airline tickets and hotel reservation.

The online travel sale service attraction is that the recent development in the field of information communication and technology and its practical application in tourism and hospitality industry. Generally , online travel sale service must have consumer side and the supplier side.

The decision making prcess of consumer was analyzed and it was found that travel information search and traveller individual electronic ticker pre paid to prebook any plane seat, hotel rooms and restaurants prices comparison to prebook service of traveler individual purchase behavior are corresponding with the usae of (ICT).

1.4 What is the online travel sale service strategy?

The two most important things for travel operators (agents) are online travel marketing and strategic management. Former can enhance business operations. Use of (ICT) develops financial capabilities , however, it depends on management choice, financial condition and position. Some researchers recommended that the usage of IT should not be restricted at operational level, however it should be extended up to senior level and should be used for decision making. Social media is regarded as a platform where the tourists and travel operators/agents (suppliers) of tourism industry cross each other. Thus, the role of social media has been directed for future research in tourism industry. Hence, it seems online travel sale service has these features to attract travel consumers to choose to use this online mode to buy electronic air ticket. Such as, airline electronic air ticket price comparison, pre-booking plan seats to avoid full seats flights to delay consumer individual trip plan, pre-booking hotel rooms and prices comparison as well as prebooking restaurant seats and food price and taste comparison, travel destination easy search. Otherwise, these features to attract travel consumers to choose to walk in to travel agents to buy paper air ticket directly. They include: safe cash or visa card payment to avoid personal information is stolen by website payment channel, e.g. via card number, address, name , birth date personal information. Also the travel consumer can enquire any questions from the travel agent and gets individual feedback from the travel agent by oral before who ensure to choose to buy which kind of travel package for whose travel destination. In special, when the travel consumer has much time to spend to enquire any travel trip question, walk in travel agent is the best enquire methods to let the travel consumer to know the trip information clearly.

Online/offline travel operators
(agents) maketing strategies

2.1 Offline walk in travel unique segment service strategy

Nowadays, online and offlce travel operators competitions are serious. In fact, tourism marketing , there will be more need for online travel operators in the future, due to online travel sale service is popular to be accepted by online travel consumers. Thus, I recommend walk in offline travel agents need to concentrate on focusing some unique travel service to attract new or old travel consumers if who hope to survive.

I recommend that they can focus on specific specialized services, such as travel consultation (specialization) hypothesizing that systematic differences exist between the usage of travel agents for different travel contexts and travel agents can survive if they focus on specific segments of the market, such as older travelers (segmentation; hypothesizing that systematic differences exist between the usage of travel agents depending on the personal characteristics of travellers). The unique travel needs include: specific services related to package holidays, transport services, beach on city holidays, as well as destinations travellers are not familiar with.

I shall give my opinions to provide insight into alternative strategies for travel agencies in a matured travel market with a high internet penetration as below:

The internet online travel sale service is a reality of popular to let travel consumers to feel convenient to pre-book air seat, hotel rooms , air electronic ticket prices comparison. In order to make final purchase decision very easily in the shortest time. Consequently , it has penetrated the decision making process of travel to attract them to choose to buy electronic air ticket, prebooking hotel rooms or restaurant seats from online travel agent channel more than walk in offline travel agent channel. This is especially true in the tourism business where consumption to consume (booking) and the purchase-related information search (Bieger & Lasesser 2004; Crotts 1998).

In fact , apply website to provide travel sale method has these good consequence. From travel operator (agent) supplier's perspective, the success potential derived from operating a website consist of lower distribution costs, higher revenues and a larger potential market share (due to the ubiquitous access). From traverler's perspective, the internet allows direct communication with tourism suppliers facilitatinf requests for information and allowing services and travel related products, e.g. prebooking hotel rooms, restaurant seats , electronic or paper air tickets, travel trip arrangement package products to be purchased at any time and any place from online travel agents /operators conveniently.

Offline / online travel agency (operator) business depends on earn commissions on behalf of airlines. Thus, offline walk in travel agency (operator) business model that would extend existence as a booking agency (thus focusing on consultation and interpersonal contact) strategy.

As a matter of fact, commission -cutting , which began in the US well ahed of Europe, has had a profound effect specially on business travel agents

. Consequently , many of them have re-invented themselves as " travel managers", instead of selling tickets and making arrangements, they charge consultancy fees for reducing the amounts client companies spend on travel (Daneshku, 1999).

2.2 Systematic differences strategy applies to offline walk in travel agent

Thus, I recommend systematic differences strategy can be applied offline walk in travel agent (operator). It means that walk in travel agents could reorient their offline walk in travel agent business to focus on contexts that are less substitutable by other channels and media . Factors hypothetically attributing to the delineation of travel contexts include: helping travellers to choose best travel destinations, helping travellers to attempt to find the number of previous trips (indicating the familiarity with a destination) for their travel reference, helping them to find the cheapest, the most convenient and the most close transportation to ctch during their trips, helping them to find the different types of accommodation and rooms price comparison , nature/type of the trip comparison , arrangement of time of booking (as indicator of spontneous / planned travel) nd helping them to budget overall travel expenditure .

Systematic differences in travel agent use exist in dependence of personal (characteristics with with tourists. Walk in offline travel agents could benefit from a travelling client segmentation strategy and customize and target their services to those travellers that are most likely to be and remain their customers.

Factors hypotheticlly attributing to the traveller segment include: travel expenditure per day, useful travel information as indicator for perceived risk and socio-demographic (age, gender, highest completed and education, professional positions) . Generally, the role of walk in offline travel agent with regard to the travel infrormation search and booking behavior have take an incoming perspective. Such as looking at visitors from different travel markets at a similar destinations. The comparison of central importance in determining whether specialization of travel contexts or market segments is the more promising strategy for walk in offline travel agents.

However, travel package tours strategy must b offline walk in travel attraction . Due to some walk in travellers target segmentation market has still needs. Generally, this travel package tours of travel segmentation consumer who like to enquire the travel agents to concern what the hotel rooms price are the cheapest to provide to them to live, what transportation tools the travel agent can arrange to them to catch anywhere the country destination, the travel agent can provide them to visit during their tour journey. Thus, the travel trip package service is still popular need to offline walk in travel agent (operator). This market is only belonged to offline walk in travel agents (operators) nowadays.

2.3 Service fees and commission cuts strategy

The reduction or removal of airline commission continues to challenge travel agencies' profitability It is crucial to understand what trends travel agencies need to be aware of to ensure how to profitability and increase travel agencies' revenues with service-fee models.

Service fees are not only a way to compensate for the loss of airline commission but also a way to generate new revenue sources for travel agencies that guarantee their long term profitability. Many travel agencies are expanding their service fee models, both in terms of the mounts changed and the number of service to airline.

However, if travel agent charge too much service fee to exceed the general airline travel market service fee reasonable or standard level. It will influence many airlines do not choose to find the travel agent to help them to sell air tickets. Travel agents apply fees most often for airline related services. They charge differentiated fees depending on the destination, type of reservation (e.g. frequent flyer), number of tickets sold or type of airline (e.g. full service versus).

However, service fee increases can raise customer loyalty and satisfaction. It won't reduce client numbers or result in a lose in clients.. The reason is that service fees can be tailored to suit individual customer. This helps travel agencies target their clients, with tailored services based on their past purchasing patterns and identity services for which clients' willingness to pay is greater , such as trip planning identity service for which pay , such as hotel only or special promotion.

To revenue mix for travel agencies is increasingly shifting to service fes as airlines have lowered or cut commissions. Successful travel agencies in many European countries are fast adopting, and constantly upgrading , their service fee schemes. Thus, it seems reasonable service fee level is one important factor to influence travel agents and airlines good relationship. In fact, even travel agents raise service fee, it won't influence travel consumer number to be reduced , even they raise air ticket price. It they can provide the informations concerning the reasonable hotel rooms prices and food quality comparison to satisfy travel consumers' living arrangement or helping them to find the reasonable restaurants' food prices and where are their location arrangement or providing the reasonable airlines' electronic air tickets or paper air tickets sale service, even arrangement any high entertainment quality of travel destination trips to let travel consumers to feel satisfactory.

However, I believe the raise air ticket price factor won't influence the travel consumer number to be decreased. Any offline or online travel agents will encounter this crisis. By cutting travel agents' commission. Airlines decreased their dependence on travel agencies as a distribution channel. In fact, three key variable factors will influence travel agents' commission income to be decreased. They include below:

- The unsustainable or no change financial losses by airlines , due to the growth of low cost carriers, leading to an increase in the number of bankruptcies.
- No negative consequences from previous commission cuts: airline had progressively lowed the commission payments.
- No effective resource for travel agencies to satisfy airlines needs.
- The appearance of now airlines and air routes to provide to travel agencies to fall down air ticket price to attract consumers' choices, due to who don't feel to spend much money to go to this new air routes or catch new airline plans , whether these new air routes are excite to entertainment or whether they are safe planes to catch.
- An increase in the number of bankruptcies to cause travel comsumption desire to be reduced.
- New competition forced down air fares.
- The necessity to cut production costs, especially with low cost meaning low production costs and low fares, even if the two are closely linked.

2.4 Internet negative influences to travel agents

Although, on the one hand, internet creates offline travel agents to use websites to help them to sell electronic air ticket or travel related products, such as prebooking hotel rooms , restaurants, transportation tools etc. travel service. However, on the other hand, internet also brings travel agencies competitive disadvantage with regad to suppliers' direct websites , when airlines are able to control seat availability and prices. Indeed internet cause the decision is made by the airlines to reduce and/or eliminate travel agency commission has led them to use technology that many of their distrust or are not inclined to use, and to compare prices and travel schedules constantly.

As a result of this travel sale service environment, traditional offline travel agencies are at a competitive disadvantage with regard to online travel agencie and to airline carriers, which have developed their own direct websites where they are able to control seat availability and prices.

Nevertheless, travel agents' pay programmes remain. From some airlines, travel agents receive negotiated incentive commission closely linked to their performance as incentive . However, airlines still need travel agents' assistance to help them to promote air tickets to sell, due to travel agents can provide trip packages, transportation tools, prebooking hotel rooms, restaurants and air tickets arrangement and they can give any enquiries to every individual travel consumer. It is free charge travel professional enquiry service for travel agency's competitive features.

Consequently, how agencies can reduce their reliance on airline commission payments. I recommend these following strategic options to them to apply as below:

- Streamlining operations, controlling staff costs, when ensuring the client feels as little impact as possible.
- Expanding or moving into the leisure business, where commissions on ono-air products remain high (cruise, hotel, railway travel)
- Specializing in geographic areas or becoming niche players for specific leisure products, e.g. destination weddings, student travel group cultural travel, cruises only, cruise and railway travel etc.
- (d) establishing a service fee driven business model.

2.5 Concentrating on business travel marketing strategy

The certain characteristics to the business travel market allowed this sector to adapt more easily to the disappearance of commission. Business travel systems have always had different relationship with different customers. They usually have long term buyer relationships, set up long before the commission cap. Some of them quickly renegotiated their contracts to include a transaction or management fee, knowing that the majority of these fee arrangements are specific the need of the client.

The reasons why airlines reduce commission to paid to travel agents. They include petrol costs increasing, e.g. indirect and by pass the established distribution chain by developing airlines' their own websites;

reducing or removing commission paid to travel agencies. Consequently, the decision to cut travel agencies' commission clearly shows that airlines wanted to decrease their reliance and dependence on travel agencies as a distribution channel. Thus, the internet appears to be an efficient and cost-effective distribution channel. Also, by creating airlines' own websites and setting directly to their clients, airlines are also to control seat availability to their clients and prices to their websites.

2.5.1 What an e-commerce strategy is used by internet travel websites?

Nowadays, the commercial use of electronic travel ticket travel is common, the most purchased online products include, for example, the name brands in online travel Epedia.travel .com and cheap tickets have been or are being integrated in large online travel firms.

Generally, online travel websites apply these strategies to attract travel consumers as below:

Firstly, shopping mall strategy, means to conduct a comprehensive factors for e-commerce. The online service provider needs to organize catalogs of services, take orders through their websites, accept payments securely, send service or related document, such as airline tickets to consumers and manage client data , such as client profiles.

Secondly, portal strategy, portal websites , such as yahoo give visitors the chance to find almost everything , they are working for in one place. Websites , such as Altavista.com and yahoo.com provide users with a shopping page that links them to many sites carrying a variety of products. Once a client is familiar with a website, who will be more likely to use the online service.

Thirdly, pricing strategy, low price is as a major competitive weapon. It includes a comparison pricing on discount price or price negotiation to let online travel consumers to get the best electronic travel ticket price choice to buy any airline tickets.

2.5.2 Travel agents vs online booking: Tackling the shortcomings and strengths

Consequently, however, one travel consumer who chooses either online booking sale service or traditional walk in offline travel agent to enquire travel service. These both of travel sale methods have shortcomings also. Such as it is possible that online electronic travel ticket purchase has personal data ,e.g. visa card, name, birth data, address, which will be stolen by online crime internet users more easily, who can not enquire any travel questions to get clear travel information concern whose travel destination package service choice or hotel room choice or transportation tool or restaurant choice and airline choice by travel agent. Also, it is possible that walk in travel agent paper travel ticket purchase shortcomings include that the travel consumer can not check any airlines' seat and pre book hotel room or transport tool or restaurant in the shorten time if who needs to fly immediately. Thus, it seems that online travel agent's client group is business travel intention, who does not need to enquire travel agent and has desire to per book airline seat in the short time. Otherwise, the offline walk in agent's client group is entertainment intention , who need to walk in to travel agent to enquire whose travel package and has no desire to pre book airline seat in the short time. Thus, online travel agent ought concentrate on design good travel package for the business travel consumers. Otherwise, offline travel agent ought concentrate on design good travel package for the entertainment travel consumers. Thus, they can have themselves unique travel target package to adopt to their different travel need. Such as business travel consumers need to live cheap and comfortable hotels, catching cheap and fast transportation tools in their business trips, eating in cheap and good taste food in restaurant and spending the less time to catch the airline plan to arrive the destination and cheap and comfortable business class plan seat. Such as entertainment travel consumers need the travel agent can help them to design cheap and enjoyable travel package, includes living comfortable hotel room, exciting and enjoyable trip, good taste food and railway, travel bus, cruise and plane provision in trip.

In conclusion, In fact, tourism is a quite unique area of business in a sense that is a travel sale service product and it can't be observed or manipulated through direct experience prior to purchase . Instead clients have to purely rely on indirect or virtual experience. Thus, every online or offline travel agent ought attempt to design different travel package to attract every business traveler or entertainment traveller trip need because every traveler will have personal unique trip need in this competitive travel sale service market in the future.

Reference

Bieger. Th., and Ch. Laesser (2004). " Information sources for travel decisions: Toward a source process model," Journal of travel reserch, 42(4):

357-371.

Daneshku, S. (1999). " Unwived travel agents unworried bi internet, " Financial Times , London. June 16, 1999:10.

Foucault, B. Lery, N. Rifkin, A. & Silfies , 2000.
" Comparision of textbook prices by retailer and by college" working paper. Cornell University, Ithaca, Ney.

CHAPTER VII

AI technology how is applied to online office working environment

Artificial intelligence bank service working environment
Focus on outcomes not technology.Artificial Intelligence: Waiting to be unleashed? The Insider Column - When Digital Transformation misses. Are you meeting the demands of the new digital consumer? Will your legacy mindset compromise your digital competitiveness? Can artificial intelligence create online remote office new business service market in global ?
The Future of Artificial Intelligence In The Workplace:
Is AI going to displace workers or come as a benefit to them?
Is AI going to displace workers or come as a benefit to them? Getty
Smart technologies aren't just changing our homes; they're edging their way into their numerous industries and are disrupting the workplace. Artificial Intelligence (AI) has the potential to improve productivity, efficiency and accuracy across an organization – but is this entirely beneficial? Many fear that the rise of AI will lead to machines and robots replacing human workers and view this progression in technology as threat rather than a tool to better ourselves.
With AI continuing to be a prominent online office service business to replace human actual office working environment, businesses need to realize that self-learning and black-box capabilities are not the panacea. Many organisations are already beginning to see the incredible capabilities of AI, using these advantages to enhance human intelligence and gain real value from their data. As there is increasing evidence demonstrating the benefits of intelligent systems, more decision-makers in the boardroom are gaining a better understanding of what AI can really offer. Research conducted by EY explains "organizations enabling AI at the enterprise level are increasing operational efficiency, making faster, more informed decisions and innovating new products and services." Can articial intelligent technology create remote office working environment to replace our traditional actual office work environment ? Can we do not need to go

to office to work , when any office staffs ,e.g. managers, clerk, etc. they can apply artificial intelligent technology and online technology to work at home, such as remote office working environment ?

The first companies employing AI systems across the board will gain competitive advantage, reduce cost of operations and remove head counts. Whilst this may be a positive from a business perspective, it is obvious why this a worry for those working in roles at risk of displacement. The introduction of these technologies will likely trigger an issue with unions and job security due to the substantial operational changes. Although AI will affect every sector in some way, not every job is at equal risk. PwC predicts a relatively low displacement of jobs (around 3%) in the first wave of automation, but this could dramatically increase up to 30% by the mid-2030's. Occupations within the transport industry could potentially be at much greater risk, whereas jobs requiring social, emotional and literary abilities are at the lowest risk of displacement.

A positive future with artificial intelligence to bring remote online office working environment chance:

Many businesses and individuals are optimistic that this AI-driven shift in the workplace will result in more jobs being created than lost. As we develop innovative technologies, AI will have a positive impact on our economy by creating jobs that require the skill set to implement new systems. 80% of respondents in the EY survey said it was the lack of these skills that was the biggest challenge when employing AI programs.

It is likely that artificial intelligence will soon replace jobs involving repetitive or basic problem-solving tasks, and even go beyond current human capability. AI systems will be making decisions instead of humans in industrial settings, customer service roles and within financial institutions. Automated decisioning will be responsible for tasks such as approving loans, deciding whether a customer should be onboarded or identifying corruption and financial crime.

Organisations will benefit from an increase in productivity as a result of greater automation, meaning more revenue will generated. This thus provides additional money to spend on supporting jobs in the services sector.Due to the vast array of jobs that could be impacted by AI, it is fundamental to address the potential pitfalls of these technologies. Business need to overcome the trust and bias issues surrounding AI by achieving an effective and successful implementation that makes it possible for everyone to benefit.

Governments must ensure that gains from AI are shared widely across society to prevent social inequality between those affected and unaffected by these developments. For example, this could be through increased investment into training. With the additional cost-savings from implementing AI systems, employers should also focus on upskilling their current employees.

To properly leverage the power of AI, we need to address the issue at an educational level, as well as in business. Education systems needs to focus on training students in roles directly associated to working with AI, including programmers and data analysts. This requires more emphasis to be put on STEM subjects (science, technology, engineering and mathematics). Also, subjects centered around building creative, social and emotional skills should be encouraged. Whilst artificial intelligence will be more productive than human workers for repetitive tasks, humans will always outperform machines in jobs requiring relationship-building and imagination. Hence, artificial intelligence will change our world both inside and outside the workplace. Instead of focusing on the fear surrounding automation, businesses need to embrace these new technologies to ensure they implement the most effective AI systems to enhance and compliment human intelligence.

Artificial Intelligence (AI) in Banking working environment

Artificial Intelligence (AI) is a fast-evolving technology, gaining popularity all around the world. Several industries have already adopted AI for various applications, getting better and smarter day by day. In the past few years, the banking sector has also become one of the leading adopters of Artificial Intelligence. Most banks and financial institutions are implementing AI to add more efficiency to their back-office and lessen security risks.

As per Statista, the AI market in the United States is forecasted to reach 7.35 billion U.S. dollars in 2018. Some major applications of AI include classification, image recognition, object identification, and automated geophysical feature detection. Speaking of banking and financial institutions, JPMorgan Chase, Wells Fargo, Bank of America, CitiBank, and other leading U.S. banks have already implemented AI in their systems, helping consumers manage their daily banking needs more efficiently.

AI technology can bring better Customer Support in bank service environment

Several pieces of evidence advocate that the customers willingly prefer self-service options which allow them to chat with a virtual assistant as if it were a live customer representative. Most leading banks have already added virtual assistants to their instant website chatbots, voice response systems, and mobile applications. Artificial Intelligence considers each interaction as a teachable moment, so the chatbots (virtual assistants) keeps getting better while understanding customers. With AI, virtual assistants can deliver better customer support. It also allows sentiment analysis, so the virtual assistant can determine when individuals are getting frustrated and instantly transfer them to a live agent.

Enhanced Banking Services

AI streamlines the banking process while giving customer service a new level of comfortability. It allows banks to meet customers' expectations with comprehensive digital support. With Artificial Intelligence, you can achieve greater precision and accuracy. From cash transfer to bills payment, cards management, and other support, AI can significantly enrich the satisfaction level of your customers. All of these operations can be easily managed through desktops, smartphones, and other mobile devices.

Scam Recognition

With an immense growth of banking fraud, scam recognition and reduction has become challenging for the banking sector. Several banks tried to identify the factors and powerful solutions but couldn't succeed. However, AI makes it easier to detect the factors involved in frauds and support investigators. It improves financial security with advanced fraud prevention tactics. Artificial Intelligence works as a real-time scam solution for the banking sector while handling complex situations and tactics. Based on advanced data crunching, AI can detect fraud by flagging unusual transactions. It also feeds back into the consumer's profile which subsequently builds a secure environment.

Advanced Data Analytics

One of the main advantages of AI is its ability to complete tedious tasks through intricate automation, resulting in better productivity. Based on a machine learning algorithm, AI can quickly consume and process a massive amount of data at an expedited level. The enormous speed brings efficiency to financial services, providing scope for personalized offerings to consumers. What's even more, AI makes faster decisions while carrying out actions quickly. With such advantages, it is nearly obvious that the majority of banks and financial institutions will adopt AI to stay competitive and deliver better customer support. However, several cons are also associated with a machine learning algorithm. As it continues to learn and grow, the decision-making capabilities may create problems in the near future.

Disadvanages of AI in Banking Sector

Artificial intelligence is also expected to massively disrupt banks and traditional financial services. Some of its disadvantages are listed below.

Highly Expensive

Production and maintenance of artificial intelligence demand huge costs since they are very complex machines. AI also consists of advanced software programs which require regular updates to meet the needs of the changing environment. In the case of critical failures, the procedure to reinstate the system and recover lost codes may require enormous time and cost.

Bad Calls

Though Artificial Intelligence can learn and improve, it still can't make judgment calls. Humans can take individual circumstances and judgment calls into account when making decisions, something that AI might never be able to do. Replacing adaptive human behavior with AI may cause irrational behavior within ecosystems of humans and things.

Distribution of Power

There is a constant fear of AI superseding or taking over the humans. Artificial intelligence can give a lot of power to the few individuals who are controlling it. Hence, AI carries the risk and takes control away from humans while dehumanizing actions in several ways.

Unemployment

Replacement of the workforce with machines can lead to wide-reaching unemployment. Moreover, if the use of AI becomes rampant, people will be highly dependent on the machines and lose their creative power. Unemployment is a socially undesirable issue. Individuals with nothing to do can lead to the devastating use of their minds. Be it banking or any other sector; Artificial intelligence can effectively increase the unemployment rate.

Artificial Intelligence delivered to wrong hands can turn out to be a serious threat to humankind. If individuals start thinking destructively, they can generate havoc with these advanced machines. The challenges introduced by the emergence of artificial intelligence revolve around several things. However, AI is a right balance of skill and emotions which is continually growing. Artificial intelligence provides banks, financial institutions, and tech companies with significant competitive advantages. Nevertheless, it can completely transform the financial sector and make it faster, but this will only be possible if the financial industry can manage the security risk of systems based on AI.

What does artificial intelligence mean for the bank service office workers?

With all these new artificial intelligence use cases comes the question of whether machines will force humans into obsolescence. The jury is still out: Some experts vehemently deny that artificial intelligence will automate so many jobs that millions of people find themselves unemployed, while other experts see it as a pressing problem.

"The structure of the workforce is changing, but I don't think artificial intelligence is essentially replacing jobs in bank service working environment. It allows us to really create a knowledge-based economy and leverage that to create better automation for a better form of life. It might be a little bit theoretical, but I think if you have to worry about artificial intelligence and robots replacing some bank service jobs, e.g. bank security, bank enquiry service,. But, AI can not replace bank counter service staffs to do saving or withdrawing money transfer tasks when any customers prepare to save money or withdraw money in bank counters. As this technology develops, the AI bank service will see new startups, numerous saving or withdraw transactions from consumer won't be raise more easily.

AI to Banking and Finance industry

The banking and finance industry plays a major role in our lives. I mean the world runs on money and banks are essentially the gatekeepers that regulate that flow. Did you know that the banking and finance industry heavily relies on artificial intelligence for things like customer service, fraud protection, investment, and more? A simple example is the automated emails that you receive from banks whenever you do an out of the ordinary transaction. Well, that's AI watching over your account and trying to warn you of any fraud.

AI is also being trained to look at large samples of fraud data and find a pattern so that you can be warned before it happens to you. Also, when you hitch a little snag and chat with bank's customer service, chances are that you are chatting with an AI bot. Even the big players in the finance industry use AI to analyze data to find the best avenues to invest money so they can get the most returns with the least risk. That's not all, AI is poised to play an even bigger role in the industry as major banks across the world are investing billions of dollars in the AI technology and we all will observe its effects sooner than later

How AI influences our daily working life in any office working environment

Can AI bring only disadvantages? If AI can bring disadvantges, what are its disadvantages to any working environment ?The entire tech world is debating the consequences of artificial intelligence and the part AI is going to play in shaping our future. While we might think that artificial intelligence is at least a few years away from causing any considerable effects on our lives, the fact remains that it is already having an enormous impact on us. Artificial intelligence is affecting our decisions and our lifestyles every day. Don't believe me? I shall indicate some product examples how AI anticipates which can influence our working culture in any office environment.

Examples of how Artificial Intelligence assistance to office working environment may include as below:

1. Smartphones

Smartphones have become the most indispensable tech product that we own today and we use it almost all the time. Well, if you are using a smartphone, you are interacting with AI whether you know it or not. From the obvious AI features such as the built-in smart assistants to not so obvious ones such as the portrait mode in the camera, AI is impacting our lives in every day office working environment.

In fact, the two examples that I provided that our working world of AI and how it is effecting our working lives. Firstly, there are the obvious AI elements which most of us have some knowledge about. For example, when you are using a smart assistant in office, whether it's Google Assistant, Alexa, Siri, or Bixby, you more or less know that these assistants are based on AI. However, when we are using a feature such as the portrait mode effect while shooting a picture, we never consider that AI might be behind that too. Have you ever thought how the Google Pixel phones or iPhones can capture such great portrait shots? The answer is artificial intelligence. So, when any office workers need to find any knowledge to solve their working problem immediately in any offices. They may apply AI smart phone tools to help them to apply online channel to search any new knowledge to attempt to solve their working problem in possible, when their computers have none any computers in offices.

Now more and more manufacturers are including AI in their smartphones with big chip manufacturers including Qualcomm and Huawei producing chips with built-in AI capabilities. The AI integration is helping in bringing features like scene detection, mixed and virtual reality elements, and more. AI is going to play an even major role in the coming years. We are already seeing the huge emphasis on AI with the latest Android and iOS updates. Features like app actions, splices, and adaptive battery in Android Pie and Siri shortcut and Siri suggestions in iOS 12 are made possible with AI. So, next time if any office workers think AI is not effecting them, take out your smartphone to replace computers to find any knowledge to help you to solve any tasks problems immediately in offices.

2. Social Media Feeds

If you are thinking that smart cars don't personally effect you as they are still not in your country or city, well, how about something which you use on a daily basis. Even if you are living under a rock, there's a high probability that you are tweeting from underneath it. If Twitter's not your choice of poison, maybe it's Facebook or Instagram, or Snapchat or any of the myriad of social media apps out there. Well, if you are using social media, most of your decisions are being impacted by artificial intelligence. So, any office workers may apply AI to help them to gather any new information to solve any difficult task problems , if their managers can not assist them to solve any sudden tasks problem, they are encountering to need to solve any working complex tasks problem internet social media in any any office working environment immediately.

From the feeds that office staffs can see in their working timeline to the notifications that you receive from these apps, everything is curated by AI. AI takes all your past behavior, web searches, interactions, and everything else that you do when you are on these websites and tailors the experience just for you. The sole purpose of AI here is to make the apps so addictive that you come back to them again and again, and I am ready to place a bet that AI is winning this war against you.

3. Online Ads Network

One of the biggest users of artificial intelligence is the online ad industry which uses AI to not only track user statistics but also serve us ads based on those statistics. Without AI, the online ad industry will just fail as it would show random ads to users with no connection to their preferences what so ever. AI has become so successful in determining our interests and serving us ads that the global digital ad industry has crossed 250 billion US dollars with the industry projected to cross the 300 billion mark in 2019. So next time when any product developers are going online and seeing ads or product recommendation, know that AI is impacting to any new products advertisement method more efficiently.

4. AI can be any office security

While we can all debate the ethics of using a broad surveillance system, there's no denying the fact that it is being used and AI is playing a big part in that. It is not possible for humans to keep monitoring multiple monitors with feeds from hundreds if not thousands of cameras at the same time, and hence, using AI makes perfect sense. With technologies like object recognition and facial recognition getting better and better every day, it won't be long when all the security camera feeds are being monitored by an AI and not a human. While there's still time before AI can be fully implemented such as security in any offices, this is going to be our future.

5. Smart Keyboard Apps

Smart Keyboard Apps. Granted, not everyone loves dealing with on-screen keyboards. However, they have become far more intuitive, allowing users to type comfortably and faster. What has probably proved to be a catalyst for them is the integration of AI. The smart keyboard apps keep a tab on the writing style of a user and predict words and emojis accordingly. Thus, typing on the touchscreen has become faster and more convenient. Not to mention, artificial intelligence also plays a vital role in pin-pointing misspellings and typos. So, any office workers can apply smart keyboard apps to help their to raise typing efficiency and reduce wrong typing word in error when they need to type any document in offices.

6. E-Commerce

` AI-driven algorithms have kind of given the much-needed impetus to e-commerce to provide a more personalized experience. According to several reports, its usage has vastly increased sales and also played a good part in building loyal relationships with customers. Thus, companies take advantage of AI to deploy chatbots to collect pivotal data and also predict purchases to create a customer-centric experience. Yet to come across this shift of strategy? Just spend some time with sites like Amazon and eBay and you will soon get to know how fast the landscape is changing around you – for the better! So, Ai can help any businesses to achieve e-commerce sale channel more easily.

7. Smart Email Apps

In any office working environment, if you still find your inbox cluttered with too many unwanted messages, chances are pretty high that you are still stuck with an old school email app. You heard it right! Modern email apps like Spark make the most of AI to get rid of spam messages and also categorize emails so that you can quickly access the important ones. What's more, they also offer smart replies based on the messages you receive to help you reply to any email quickly. The "Smart Reply" feature of Gmail is a great example of this. It uses AI to scan the text of the email and provides you with contextual answers. So, AI can help any office staffs to know who had sent any message from email and respond their email immediate , when AI can help any offices to avoid to receive any email spam rubbish email message in any time, even after working hours, it means that AI is working to help any office staffs to avoid to receive any email spam rubblish message in any time. So, when they go to office to work, even they go home after working hours. They can know whether what the important email messages are sent to their office email in boxes any time. Then, they can send email to respond their customers' enquires any time. So, AI can help any office workers can have chance to work at homes.

The Future of Artificial Intelligence In The Workplace

Smart technologies aren't just changing our homes; they're edging their way into their numerous industries and are disrupting the workplace. Artificial Intelligence (AI) has the potential to improve productivity, efficiency and accuracy across an organization – but is this entirely beneficial? Many fear that the rise of AI will lead to machines and robots replacing human workers and view this progression in technology as threat rather than a tool to better ourselves.

With AI continuing to be a prominent buzzword in 2019, businesses need to realize that self-learning and black-box capabilities are not the panacea. Many organisations are already beginning to see the incredible capabilities of AI, using these advantages to enhance human intelligence and gain real value from their data. As there is increasing evidence demonstrating the benefits of intelligent systems, more decision-makers in the boardroom are gaining a better understanding of what AI can really offer. Research conducted by EY explains "organizations enabling AI at the enterprise level are increasing operational efficiency, making faster, more informed decisions and innovating new products and services."

Today In: Cybersecurity

The first companies employing AI systems across the board will gain competitive advantage, reduce cost of operations and remove head counts. Whilst this may be a positive from a business perspective, it is obvious why this a worry for those working in roles at risk of displacement. The introduction of these technologies will likely trigger an issue with unions and job security due to the substantial operational changes. Although AI will affect every sector in some way, not every job is at equal risk. PwC predicts a relatively low displacement of jobs (around 3%) in the first wave of automation, but this could dramatically increase up to 30% by the mid-2030's. Occupations within the transport industry could potentially be at much greater risk, whereas jobs requiring social, emotional and literary abilities are at the lowest risk of displacement.

A positive future with artificial intelligence

Many businesses and individuals are optimistic that this AI-driven shift in the workplace will result in more jobs being created than lost. As we develop innovative technologies, AI will have a positive impact on our economy by creating jobs that require the skill set to implement new systems. 80% of respondents in the EY survey said it was the lack of these skills that was the biggest challenge when employing AI programs. It is likely that artificial intelligence will soon replace jobs involving repetitive or basic problem-solving tasks, and even go beyond current human capability. AI systems will be making decisions instead of humans in industrial settings, customer service roles and within financial institutions. Automated decisioning will be responsible for tasks such as approving loans, deciding whether a customer should be onboarded or identifying corruption and financial crime. Organisations will benefit from an increase in productivity as a result of greater automation, meaning more revenue will generated. This thus provides additional money to spend on supporting jobs in the services sector.

How to take advantage of AI to any offices

Due to the vast array of jobs that could be impacted by AI, it is fundamental to address the potential pitfalls of these technologies. Business need to overcome the trust and bias issues surrounding AI by achieving an effective and successful implementation that makes it possible for everyone to benefit. Governments must ensure that gains from AI are shared widely across society to prevent social inequality between those affected and unaffected by these developments. For example, this could be through increased investment into training.With the additional cost-savings from implementing AI systems, employers should also focus on upskilling their current employees.

To properly leverage the power of AI, we need to address the issue at an educational level, as well as in business. Education systems needs to focus on training students in roles directly associated to working with AI, including programmers and data analysts. This requires more emphasis to be put on STEM subjects (science, technology, engineering and mathematics). Also, subjects centered around building creative, social and emotional skills should be encouraged. Whilst artificial intelligence will be more productive than human workers for repetitive tasks, humans will always outperform machines in jobs requiring relationship-building and imagination. Artificial intelligence will change our world both inside and outside the workplace. Instead of focusing on the fear surrounding automation, businesses need to embrace these new technologies to ensure they implement the most effective AI systems to enhance and compliment human intelligence

How AI can help office workers to do tasks more easily

Companies are currently spending big on artificial intelligence and machine learning initiatives to the tune of $12 billion, but estimates put that figure as high as $57.6 billion by 2021, according to the International Data Corporation (IDC). With such massive shifts, the focus is usually on what we might lose, but it shouldn't be. A recent report on the future of work from the McKinsey Global Institute suggests that while only about 5% of jobs can be completely eliminated by automation, the rise of AI requires workers to beef up both technical and soft skills in order to stay competitive.

What's seldom discussed is how AI can revolutionize our jobs. It's now possible to pinpoint peak productivity for a single day, improve communication in meetings (even before people ever work together face to face), or even teach you to be a better leader, all thanks to AI platforms. I shall indicate these advantages to bring any office benefits from AI assistance as below:

1. AI can help any companies to get better to hire the best applicants

AI has the greatest potential to change the way companies find candidates, according to Alexander Rinke, cofounder and CEO of Celonis. The company's process-mining technology helps businesses to understand the areas where automation can help humans, he says. In HR departments, Celonis can help identify how fast workers come and go, the cost per hire, and which positions take the longest to fill. AI helped enable one customer's ability to identify bottlenecks in recruitment and reduced process costs internally by 30% as well as get them hired more quickly, he says.

Crafting a resume has never been easier, nor has landing an interview. Another example is how recruitment software provider iCIMS, in partnership with Google, is helping job seekers find jobs directly through the search engine, thanks to Google's AI and machine learning capabilities. Susan Vitale, iCIMS's chief marketing officer says that in addition to reducing the number of expired job postings, machine learning is underlying a private beta program of Google's Cloud Jobs Discovery model. "For a candidate searching for, say, a CTO role, Cloud Job Discovery will serve up CTO positions as well as jobs with titles that are similar, but not verbatim, such as chief technology officer or chief technical officer," says Vitale. This model also allows for conceptual search results, such as serving up job listings for cashiers, sales associates, and store associates when someone searches for one versus just only showing jobs that exactly match the keyword search criteria, she adds.

2. AI can help any office workers to raise much more productive efficiencies

John Furneaux, CEO and cofounder of Hive, says predictive analytics will help us better understand how we work. "It can tell us just about everything we want to know about teams and collaboration, for example, if men or women get more done in the afternoon, and if summer Fridays are a myth," he says. (Everyone thinks summer Fridays aren't productive, but in reality there's no difference between those and other Fridays during the year–productivity is equally low.)

Using a data set of over 30,000 completed actions across Hive workspaces, Furneaux says they were able to identify some notable trends in productivity. For example, men were far more productive early in the day, with a sharp decline in the afternoon, while women had a slower start to the day but were far more productive in later hours than their male counterparts. And analyzing chat messages revealed that women appear to complete more tasks when chatting, suggesting they use communication as a key tool to completing work. Similarly, Nintex Hawkeye analyzes data on business processes by types, users, roles, and departments to see who's doing the work and how long it takes them to do it. Management can monitor and analyze those metrics in real time.

3. AI can help any managers to make the most fair compensation and eliminate wage gaps to every staffs

Tanya Jansen, cofounder of the compensation management platform beqom, says that AI and predictive analytics can eliminate unconscious bias from compensation. Jansen says that AI based on a variety of rules including education, experience, certifications, and more can make compensation more fair and help businesses move closer to closing pay gaps. "Specifically, AI can help solve gender pay gaps and the CEO-to-worker pay gap, in which pay ratios of Fortune 500 companies range from 2:1 at the low end to nearly 5000:1 at the high end," she says. Additionally, the use of AI-driven compensation technology to make pay more fair can mitigate the risk of employee turnover, which costs businesses as much as 33% of a worker's annual salary to replace them.

4. AI can help any office staffs to arrange better meetings

Augmented Reality (AR) is still in its infancy, but AI and machine learning are the core components that make it work. As such, Christa Manning, the vice president and solution provider research leader at Bersin, Deloitte Consulting LLP, says that AR can help workers find the right information, in the right place, at the right time to make the best decisions wherever they may be working. For example, as more companies adopt video meetings and collaborative workspaces, it's likely we'll begin to see HR-curated information like talent profiles and work styles layered over interactions through AR."Imagine being in a video conference with a colleague and having direct insight into their communication style, seeing tips on how to best interact with them or reminders of what needs to be discussed. SO, AI can help any organizations to conclude or find the best methods to solve any problems after their every discussion in any meetings.

How AI is improving onboarding and training. AI coaching tools first learn by observing how different employees conduct specific tasks. Then these tools can walk new employees through how to complete those tasks—or even coach existing employees on how to do things more effectively or efficiently. Chorus is a great example of this technology. It analyzes sales calls while they happen, offering tips to help sales reps manage the cadence of meetings and use the most effective messaging. It also records all sales calls and compiles statistics for each sales rep, providing everyone with the tools they need to help them close more deals and conduct more effective calls. Another example is Cogito, a tool that combines AI with behavioral science to help customer service employees provide better phone support. It monitors calls for voice signals, providing real-time suggestions to representatives on how to improve the conversation.

5. AI can help any managers to be better leaders

Indiggo, a platform powered by a proprietary AI tool called "indi," functions as a brain that has consumed all the knowledge the company has gathered in its 15 years of operation. It also uses an algorithm to provide an estimate of how much time is wasted by a company by analyzing the size of its management team. Then it taps their calendars to see how they spend their time, and walks individual managers through a type of Q&A to make sure they are clear on what their top three priorities are, and how that relates to the organization's priorities, which will indicate if that strategy is moving forward or not. "The counterintuitive impact of these advances is that they actually make human work truly irreplaceable," Alexander Rinke, the cofounder and CEO of Celonis says. As such, he reminds us, "Humans are much better at processes that involve reasoning, judgment, and interaction with people." So, AI can recommend more accurate and useful opinions to help any managers to solve their managing challenges in office any time.

How AI is eliminating repetitive administrative tasks

There are a lot of tasks that knowledge workers spend time on that provide little—if any—value.For example, say you need to schedule a meeting to get consensus on a decision before moving forward, but you need five people to join the meeting. It's easy to spend a ton of time sending email back-and-forth or finding an open slot on everyone's calendar.That's not the most rewarding use of your time for you or your company.Tools like X.ai give employees AI-powered personal assistants that perform administrative tasks like scheduling, rescheduling, and cancelling meetings.

How AI is transforming internal communications and support

Personnel on the teams that provide employee support have their hands full with other responsibilities, too. HR teams work on building the kind of company people love working for. IT maintains the company's network and keeps data secure. Office managers frequently run big events like holiday parties.These tasks are crucial, but they're often hard for teams to focus on because they're busy answering routine questions. AI service desks like askSpoke allow employee support teams to balance their service commitments with other important responsibilities by reducing interruptions from rote, repetitive requests.Employees can askSpoke for whatever they need over Slack, email, SMS, and the web. askSpoke's friendly AI will automatically provide a prompt response.

How AI is transforming marketing, sales, and customer service

AI-powered chatbots help with external support as well. Just like with internal support tools like askSpoke, these chatbots learn from real marketers, salespeople, and customer service reps and are eventually able to answer questions as accurately as a knowledgeable person.For example, chatbot for Messenger helps customers plan their vacations. It books flights, hotels, and cars, highlights destination attractions, and even provides answers to questions like "Where can I go for $100 expense budget only?"

How AI is transforming business data and analytics

It's hard to run a competitive business today without data. But even massive amounts of data are useless without a way to transform that data into valuable insights. That's typically why you'd want to hire a data scientist—which just happens to be one of the most difficult roles to fill. How AI is fighting fraud and transforming security. Have you ever taken a call from your bank to find that someone used your debit card fraudulently? Most likely, your bank used some form of AI to detect the fraudulent transaction and decline it. Applying the same basic technology to the workplace helps identify security risks and keeps customer, employee, and company data safe. AI-powered software can automatically detect and address threats among thousands or millions of signals that humans would never be able to parse (especially not in real-time).

How AI is transforming productivity

While AI is transforming the workplace in many different ways across every industry, it's impacting productivity most of all. When your office staffs don't have to scroll through calendars to look for open meeting times, build reports in spreadsheets to look for insights, or spend your day answering the same questions over and over again, you're more productive. Workers are freed from redundant and mindless tasks, giving them more time to do work that matters, solve problems, and exercise their creativity. Some tools use AI to specifically monitor and boost productivity. For example, Deloitte's LaborWise provides company leaders and managers with productivity analytics that help them identify areas where labor costs are too high, impediments that slow people down, and departments that need additional staff.

In conclusion, what AI means for the workplace of the future. While some will dramatize the negative impacts of AI, cognitive computing, and robotics, these powerful tools will also help create new jobs, boost productivity, and allow workers to focus on the human aspects of work. Essentially, automation frees companies and their employees up to be more empathetic, to focus on things like the customer experience, employee engagement, and workplace culture.

What are traditional office tools to be replaced by AI ?
Artificial intelligence (AI) is predicted to eliminate over a million jobs in the next few years, potentially replacing lower level positions like administrative assistants with humanoid robots or voice assistants. But in the nearer future, fresh AI-driven software and products are also moving to eliminate non-human elements of the workplace by replacing traditional office tools, including both physical products and everyday electronic processes. Why should businesses switch from the tried-and-true to emerging technology? Many of the experts TechRepublic talked to said the AI options streamline business practices, making their adopters work smarter instead of harder. I shall indicate these office tools ,they can be applied to help any office staffs to finish their these tasks in office, they may include as below:

1. Scheduling
Workloud's end-to-end, cloud-based workforce management software takes scheduling from paper or Excel and moves it to the cloud. Everything from clocking in and out to monitoring employee absences is fully digitalized.Schedules and timesheets are accurate, created easily, and accessible through the service's web, tablet, and mobile apps. The software can also be used for absence management.

2. Employee talent selection
Using AI and organizational behavior science, can be used to replace internal spreadsheets and databases designed to monitor human capital. By mining employee attributes and experiences, the software can recommend who would be best for a project. The software also collects reviews after projects to better predict successful employee-project matches.The traditional hiring process is slow, biased and inaccurate, By removing humans from the beginning stages of the process, it can become faster and more fair, and result in better hires.
AI software automates the hiring process, using online simulations instead of manual screenings and interviews. Using the software, employers can include tasks in a job application, allowing job candidates to show technical skills that may be necessary for a job. Employers can't rule out candidates until they see how the candidate performs, eliminating bias that occurs in the resume reading stage. Both sides also automatically receive updates about each other's steps, reducing the amount of time it takes to .

3.Timesheets: Allocate
Using AI and machine learning, the software registers an employee's

computer activity throughout the day. The data, which can also pull information from email and calendars, is used to suggest timesheet entries to reflect a more accurate amount of time an employee spent working. The employee can review and revise as necessary. However, the software doesn't spy on or monitor employees. The data is only available to each employee, while others in the company can only see the timesheet's output, which Allocate said would be the same information available if a manual sheet was used. So,replacing manual timesheets with Allocate has three advantages: More accurate time entry, project analytics, and "'unsucking' the work experience."

4. Document storage

By using AI to read and analyze business and legal documents, AI can store all of the important document-based information in the cloud. The severe reduction in print-outs means less paper and ink, fewer products like binder clips and boxes to store and organize all of the paper, and more employee time freed up from not needing to manually sort through every document. For example, in any lawyer offices, legal professionals' morale in the industry can suffer when they are pushed into performing such dull, repetitive tasks like sorting through and coding documents by hand, With AI tools to automate those duties, lawyers can focus on more meaningful projects and boost the business's and clients' success as a result. While focused on law firms, businesses that have a lot of unstructured data in documents may also be able to use the service to free up employee time and save on printing costs.

5. Scanners: Adobe Scan

While documents are moving to the cloud more and more, sometimes a physical copy of a document still needs to be scanned using a bulky office scanner. Adobe Scan, an app that condenses a scanner to the size of a smartphone, can rid offices of the need for an in-house scanner. Users can download and open the app, then hold their device over whatever they need to scan. Adobe Sensei then turns the scan into a PDF, and sends it to the Adobe Document Cloud. The app can transform any image into digital text that can then be searched and used electronically. The app streamlines the scanning process, making scans cleaner and more immediate. For businesses already using Adobe services, the app makes documents easily accessible.

6. Landline phones

While landlines in homes are increasingly less common, the same cannot be said for offices. But using chatbots and AI integrations, RingCentral is trying to replace traditional office landline phone systems. The platform offers over 100 integrations, including that AI landline phones can let employees check their voicemail, and a Gong.io option that listens to call recordings to find traits of successful employees than can be used in training. An add-on for Gmail lets users switch from emailing back and forth to a voice session without needing to look up contact information. AI landline phone is easy to adopt and use in the workplace, and is more customizable than standard phone systems, said David Lee, vice president of platform products. Compared to the traditional option, the cloud-based option is "future-proof.

How artificial intelligence can raise office efficiency

Artificial Intelligence is already impacting every industry through automation and machine learning, bringing concerns that AI is on the fast track to replacing many jobs. But these fears aren't new, says Dan Jackson, director of Enterprise Technology at Crestron, a company that designs workplace technology. "I'd argue this is no different than when we moved from an agricultural to an industrial economy at the turn of the last century. The percentage of people working in agriculture significantly decreased, and it was a big shift, but we still have plenty of jobs 100 years later," he says. Anytime society experiences a major technological advancement, we need to be prepared for it to change the way we live and work. It's hard to imagine what the future of jobs will look like with AI, but that future exists. And optimists suggest that, like the sewing machine to the textile industry, AI will make us better, more efficient and faster workers.

In fact, many experts agree that AI has the potential to eliminate mundane, administrative work, while we will always rely on human workers to be empathetic, collaborative, creative and strategic. But it's impact on any industry lies in the hands of the business leaders who are responsible for adopting AI strategies.

● Training presents challenges

A recent study of 1,000 global companies by Accenture found that AI is already creating three new categories of jobs: trainers, explainers and sustainers. Trainers are the people who teach AI systems how to act -- whether it's language, human behavior or the intricacies of human interaction. Explainers are the liaison between technology and business leaders, providing more insight and clarity into machine learning for the non-tech workers. Sustainers are the workers required to maintain AI systems and troubleshoot any potential issues. Some jobs were highly technical and required advanced degrees, but other roles demanded innately human things such as empathy and interaction. Downstream jobs, such as those in sales, marketing, or service will change to take advantage of the insights from AI, but many of the core skills will remain. However, it might sound like any job related to AI will require years of technical knowledge, but that isn't the case. We've already seen a shift in tech hiring -- companies often need highly specific skill sets that are hard to find in potential candidates. As a result, more businesses are hiring employees with the right soft skills, and then training them in technical skills.

An office effort measured approach to AI

The real takeaway is that any approach to AI will need to consider the human aspect of every business. AI has great potential to increase efficiency and accuracy and it's already been proven in certain industries. For example, the use of AI In banking to identify and money laundering schemes. It's also improved healthcare by "increasing the speed and accuracy" of cancer diagnosistics. AI can also help reduce the cost and length of human trafficking investigations, a situation where time is precious. In these examples, AI hasn't replaced jobs, but has positively impacted efficiency.

Thus, we need to ensure our education system responds to equip young people with the appropriate skills and adaptability, while businesses and public organizations must invest in training. Perhaps most of all, we need to encourage imagination and willingness to experiment. The organizations that can innovate with AI will reap the benefits. Their growth will make them the primary source of future jobs. Companies have a choice when implementing AI. They can choose to effectively implement systems that make employee's lives easier and find creative ways to leverage the technology. It's up to employers to ease fears for workers around AI and build strategies that benefit everyone. Hence, some AI experts believe AI can only raise efficiency to some office tasks, however, AI can not still raise efficiency to all office tasks for any office deparments. The reasons are because some office tasks which can only dominate to finish by human office workers. These office tasks are as below:

How can leaders and managers improve employee productivity while still saving time? These below tasks, AI experts ensure that AI can not help any office workers to raise their efficiencies as below:

1. Office managers can not delegate to AI to help them to do. While this tip might seem the most obvious, it is often the most difficult to put

into practice. We get it–your company is your baby, so you want to have a direct hand in everything that goes on with it. While there is nothing wrong with prioritizing quality (it is what makes a business successful, after all), checking over every small detail yourself rather than delegating can waste everyone's valuable time. Instead, give responsibilities to qualified employees, and trust that they will perform the tasks well. This gives your employees the opportunity to gain skills and leadership experience that will ultimately benefit your company. You hired them for a reason, now give them a chance to prove you right.

2. Office managers can not match Tasks to Skills to AI. Knowing your employees' skills and behavioral styles is essential for maximizing efficiency. For example, an extroverted, creative, out-of-the-box thinker is probably a great person to pitch ideas to clients. However, they might struggle if they are given a more rule-intensive, detail-oriented task. Asking your employees to be great at everything just isn't efficient–instead, before giving an employee an assignment, ask yourself: is this the person best suited to perform this task? If not, find someone else whose skills and styles match your needs.

3. Office managers can not teach AI to replace them how to communicate and teach their low level staffs how to work effectively. Every manager knows that communication is the key to a productive workforce. Technology has allowed us to contact each other with the mere click of a button (or should we say, tap of a touch screen)–this naturally means that current communication methods are as efficient as possible, right? Not necessarily. A McKinsey study found that emails can take up nearly 28% of an employee's time. In fact, email was revealed to be the second most time-consuming activity for workers (after their job-specific tasks). Instead of relying solely on email, try social networking tools (such as Slack) designed for even quicker team communication. You can also encourage your employees to occasionally adopt a more antiquated form of contact...voice-to-voice communication. Having a quick meeting or phone call can settle a matter that might have taken hours of back-and-forth emails. All of above communication tasks, I believe that AI can not do better than managers in offices.

4. AI can not keep Goals Clear and focused to be better than managers. You can't expect employees to be efficient if they don't have a focused goal to aim for. If a goal is not clearly defined and actually achievable, employees

will be less productive. So, try to make sure employees' assignments are as clear and narrow as possible. Let them know exactly what you expect of them, and tell them specifically what impact this assignment will have. One way to do this is to make sure your goals are "SMART" – specific, measurable, attainable, realistic, and timely. Before assigning an employee a task, ask yourself if it fits each of these requirements. If not, ask yourself how the task can be tweaked to help your workers stay focused and efficient.

5. AI can not know how to incentivize Employees to work more efficiently. One of the best ways to encourage employees to be more efficient is to actually give them a reason to do so. Recognizing your workers for a job well done will make them feel appreciated and encourage them to continue increasing their productivity. When deciding how to reward efficient employees, make sure you take into account their individual needs or preferences. For example, one employee might appreciate public recognition, while another would prefer a private "thank you." In addition to simple words of gratitude, here are a few incentives managers can know how to incentivize their staffs to work efficiently, but AI is only one machine, it can not perform very good.

6. AI does not know how to assist managers to train and Develop employees. Reducing training, or cutting it all together, might seem like a good way to save company time and money (learning on the job is said to be an effective way to train, after all). However, this could ultimately backfire. Forcing employees to learn their jobs on the fly can be extremely inefficient.
So, instead of having workers haphazardly trying to accomplish a task with zero guidance, take the extra day to teach them the necessary skills to do their job. This way, they can set about accomplishing their tasks on their own, and your time won't be wasted down the road answering simple questions or correcting errors. Past their original training, encourage continued employee development. Helping them expand their skillsets will build a much more advanced workforce, which will benefit your company in the long run. There are a number of ways you can support employee development: individual coaching, workshops, courses, seminars, shadowing or mentoring, or even just increasing their responsibilities. Offering these opportunities will give employees additional skills that allow them to improve their efficiency and productivity. But, AI do not know how

to improve any office workers' performance more easily than managers.

- How can AI be dangerous to office working environment?

Most researchers agree that a superintelligent AI is unlikely to exhibit human emotions like love or hate, and that there is no reason to expect AI to become intentionally benevolent or malevolent. Instead, when considering how AI might become a risk to any office working environments, experts think two scenarios most likely:

The AI is programmed to do something devastating: Autonomous weapons are artificial intelligence systems that are programmed to kill. In the hands of the wrong person, these weapons could easily cause mass casualties. Moreover, an AI arms race could inadvertently lead to an AI war that also results in mass casualties. To avoid being thwarted by the enemy, these weapons would be designed to be extremely difficult to simply "turn off," so humans could plausibly lose control of such a situation. This risk is one that's present even with narrow AI, but grows as levels of AI intelligence and autonomy increase. So, if some businessmen apply AI to be business weapon to attack or steal their business competitors' business secret, e.g. contract document, employee performance report, profit report, even business secret document. Then, AI will be one business competitor weapon more than business assistant role in any business market. So, whether AI is office assistant or business competitor weapon, it depends on how the businessmen apply them to assist their business development.

The AI is programmed to do something beneficial, but it develops a destructive method for achieving its goal: This can happen whenever we fail to fully align the AI's goals with ours, which is strikingly difficult. If you ask an obedient intelligent car to take you to the airport as fast as possible, it might get you there chased by helicopters and covered in vomit, doing not what you wanted but literally what you asked for. If a superintelligent system is tasked with a ambitious geoengineering project, it might wreak havoc with our ecosystem as a side effect, and view human attempts to stop it as a threat to be met.

As these examples illustrate, the concern about advanced AI isn't malevolence but competence. A super-intelligent AI will be extremely good at accomplishing its goals, and if those goals aren't aligned with ours, we have a problem. You're probably not an evil ant-hater who steps on ants out of malice, but if you're in charge of a hydroelectric green energy project and there's an anthill in the region to be flooded, too bad for the ants. A key goal of AI safety research is to never place humanity in the position of those ants. Because AI has the potential to become more intelligent than any human, we have no surefire way of predicting how it will behave. We can't use past technological developments as much of a basis because we've never created anything that has the ability to, wittingly or unwittingly, outsmart us. The best example of what we could face may be our own evolution. People now control the planet, not because we're the strongest, fastest or biggest, but because we're the smartest. If we're no longer the smartest, are we assured to remain in control?

A captivating conversation is taking place about the future of artificial intelligence and what it will/should mean for humanity. There are fascinating controversies where the world's leading experts disagree, such as: AI's future impact on the job market; if/when human-level AI will be developed; whether this will lead to an intelligence explosion; and whether this is something we should welcome or fear. But there are also many examples of of boring pseudo-controversies caused by people misunderstanding and talking past each other. To help ourselves focus on the interesting controversies and open questions — and not on the misunderstandings — let's clear up some of the most common myths.

There have been a number of surveys asking AI researchers how many years from now they think we'll have human-level AI with at least 50% probability. All these surveys have the same conclusion: the world's leading experts disagree, so we simply don't know. For example, in such a poll of the AI researchers at the 2015 Puerto Rico AI conference, the average (median) answer was by year 2045, but some researchers guessed hundreds of years or more. There's also a related myth that people who worry about AI think it's only a few years away. In fact, most people on record worrying about superhuman AI guess it's still at least decades away. But they argue that as long as we're not 100% sure that it won't happen this century, it's smart to start safety research now to prepare for the eventuality. Many of the safety problems associated with human-level AI are so hard that they may take decades to solve. So, any businessmen ought have business moralty to know whether they ought how to apply their AI to assist their business development in our future office environment to be more moral.

- Five ways to use AI to improve business efficiency to these office tasks

Regardless of a company's size or type, its executives typically look for ways to help it operate as efficiently as possible. They understand the link between efficiency and profitability. If employees waste too much time with drawn-out processes or complicated tasks, it'll be hard for the enterprise to remain profitable and adapt to challenges. Fortunately, artificial intelligence (AI) supports the need for effective business operations. Here are five ways enterprises can use AI for help: 5 ways to use AI to improve business efficiency image.Getting the best results from AI means looking at where bottlenecks exist, then figuring out if and how it might remove or minimise them. AI can help any offices to improve or raise efficiency to these tasks aspects as below:

1. Use AI to answer queries and support customer engagement

Chatbots are an increasingly popular option for businesses to try, and they use AI to work. Companies often build chatbots that can answer any questions from customers that come through outside of business hours. Some identify the nature of a person's problem, then either attempt to tackle it with preprogrammed answers or pass the communications to a human support worker. The retail industry, in particular, saw success by deploying chatbots. Global data collected by Juniper Research shows an estimated 2.6 billion retail-based chatbot interactions in 2019, and the company forecasts the number to rise to 22 billion in 2023.

Chatbots are excellent for answering simple questions like "How late are you open today?" or "Do you have gluten-free menu options?" Getting quick answers to queries like those increases the chances customers will choose to do business with one company over another. Equally importantly, when chatbots can give responses in a matter of seconds, there's no need for humans to stop what they're doing and address the questions.

2. To enhance reporting speed and accuracy

Company reports reveal things such as which products are selling the fastest and where they're most popular. They can also confirm the impacts of marketing campaigns on product sales, break down the costs of a new packaging choice or shipping method, and much more. However, as anyone that files reports knows, creating them is a painstaking task, and trying to rush through the process could cause mistakes. Some forward-thinking companies are combining AI with big data analytics. Doing this brings better forecasts and takes some of the burdens off the people who prepare the reports. AI also helps conquer the inevitability of mistakes. Even the most careful people make blunders, often because of mental fatigue.

AI learns to spot patterns in data and gets smarter with time. This means reports get finished faster and contain more-reliable information. The reliability aspect is crucial, especially since recently published research indicated two-thirds of the senior executives polled had no confidence or trust in big data. Using AI does not mean companies can do without data scientists. However, depending on the technology allows them to reduce the uncertainty that may otherwise exist. It also prevents employees who work with a company's data from being asked to recheck the findings, even if they initially took appropriate precautions to ensure accuracy.

3. To improve data transfer speeds

Fast data transfers help AI technology work. Concerning some information-intensive applications like virtual reality (VR), any slow transmissions greatly interfere with the realism, and content immersion people should enjoy after strapping on a VR headset. As it turns out, AI can improve data transfer speeds, too. For example, services exist that boost speeds across any wide-area network (WAN). Users enjoy consistently accelerated rates regardless of the kind of information transferred. Some companies have solutions that can reduce WAN job times by up to 98%. These AI-driven options work particularly well when companies need to move information between data centres or cloud environments.

4. To assist the IT team with identifying genuine cyberthreats and anomalies

One of the ongoing challenges faced by IT teams of all sizes is to separate the true cyber threats from false alarms. The difficulties associated with categorising the two types may mean cybersecurity professionals waste time getting to the bottom of things that are ultimately nonissues. They might miss the actual threats that could derail a company's operations. Besides detecting possible intrusions associated with a network, AI can screen for software abnormalities that may make it easier for cybercriminals to orchestrate their attacks successfully. It can also find malicious software hackers installed. Due to this kind of information and the advantages of receiving it through real-time updates, IT security teams can work more productively. They can use the majority of their resources on the threats that matter most to the company's stability.

Some organisations have even used AI to help them conquer the substantial skills shortage in the cybersecurity industry. At Texas A&M University, the Security Operations Center deals with about a million attempted hacks each month. The facility has some full-time workers, but students comprise most of the staff. They work alongside AI that aids in threat monitoring, detection and remediation. Before students see possible threats, the smart technology finds and groups them. This approach saves time and lets the team get to work investigating the problems and deciding how to handle them.

5. To streamline the time-to-hire metric when filling new positions

Statistics show the average time required to hire a person for an open position ranges from 12.7 to 49 days, depending on the industry. The timing also varies based on the type of work a job requires. For example, it takes a shorter amount of time overall to find someone for an administrative or human resources position than one associated with a creative or advertising role. Then, of course, interviews are more extensive for high-profile work.

Human resources professionals increasingly use AI to cut down on the time between first posting a job and finding the ideal individual to hire. For example, an AI platform could look for particular desired keywords in submitted resumes, saving hiring managers from poring over the documents themselves. AI can also pitch in during interviews. A company called VCV recently raised $1.7m to further develop its AI tool that has voice and facial recognition components. Candidates are asked to record videos of them answering interview questions, but they can't prepare for the specific content in advance.

In conclusion, AI Can Boost Efficiency at All Types of Companies. The examples here highlight why so many company leaders conclude that if they use AI, they could cut down on inefficiencies. Getting the best results from AI means looking at where bottlenecks exist, then figuring out if and how it might remove or minimise them. But, AI still lack enough effort to help all staffs to raise efficiency to all department tasks in any office environments.

- How the office energy Department is using AI to solve some of their office staffs electricity toughest challenges in their office working environment.

Insights from artifical intelligence has the potential to transform nearly every aspect of the world as we know it. Today, it is being applied to accelerate the pace of discovery in a wide variety of areas including energy, materials science, health care, national security, emergency response, transportation, and more. AI can be trained to help any energy department to gather data to avoid energy waste to be used to any organizations. So, AI is such as one super machine to do more accurate judgement to help any energy scientists to find the best methods to help any organizations to avoid to waste to use any energy daily. Then, organizations can avoid to spend too much energy to use in offices and they can save more money and avoid energy shortage challenge causes more easily. When the office managers can apply AI ability to reason and put it into a more automated format in a computer system to their every staffs' computer and record their computer electricity use record in their offices every day.

How can AI help offices to save energy or avoid to waste energy ?

The next industrial revolution is already happening. Artificial intelligence (AI) is ushering in an era of technologies that are faster, more adaptable, more efficient, and making the world more digitally connected. AI is best described as complementary to human intelligence, delivering the computing power to crunch numbers too big for people and recognize patterns too tedious for the human eye. In a Harvard Business Review study of 1,500 companies, it was found that the most significant performance improvements were made when humans and machines worked together. As AI becomes one of society's greatest assets, it's especially helpful for solving problems that seem larger than life — like protecting our natural environment.

Through machine learning, robotics, drones, and the internet of things (IoT), society can achieve better monitoring, understanding, and prevention of damage and stressors on Earth's land, air, and water. Even technology already available today could reduce energy usage in the U.S. by 12 to 22 percent, according to The Information Technology Industry Council (ITI). In the face of this dire reality, the potential of technology to help meet this challenge is a rare source of optimism. According to a recent survey by Intel and the research firm Concentrix, 74 percent of business-decision makers working in environmental sustainability agree artificial intelligence (AI) will help solve long-standing environmental challenges; 64 percent agree the Internet of Things (IoT) will help solve these challenges. As the field of AI develops, so will the potential to protect the environment. From the land and air to both drinking and ocean water, AI is shaping up to be the key that governments, organizations, and individuals can tap to work toward a cleaner planet, even AI can help offices to avoid to waste energy when staffs are working in offices every day.

Many AI scientists indicate that AI will also make renewable energy technology like solar panels and wind turbines more efficient and cost effective, helping them to become ubiquitous and lower society's dependence on fossil fuels. AI will also make renewable energy technology like solar panels and wind turbines more efficient and cost effective, helping them to become ubiquitous and lower society's dependence on the fossil fuels polluting the air — then hopefully eliminate them all together. Combined with the smart grid, another technology that will be enabled by

AI, this will truly progress the way people receive and use electricity in their homes, offices, and everywhere else. Smart meters save energy by allowing for two-way communication between the grid and anything that uses electricity, giving energy providers a better understanding of usage and the ability to make real-time adjustments for efficiency. Customers will benefit from the real-time data too; seeing the increased costs at peak times will encourage them to voluntarily adjust their usage to save money. This will, in turn, save even more energy: a win-win. Plus, the process of delivering the energy itself will also be improved by the smart grid, thanks to Volt/VAR control systems that can reduce the amount of energy wasted when it's in electricity transmission lines.

Can AI replace office workers

Can AI replace all office workers to do their different tasks in office different department ? If AI can only replace some department office workers to do their simple tasks, how it can raise more efficiency to compare them in some business office environments. I shall indicate some office tasks to explain how AI can help these businesses to raise their efficiency in officesas below:

- AI insurance workers

Nowadays, some country offices begin apply robotics to replace human office workers in their companies. For example, Japanese company replaces office workers with artificial intelligence in insurance industry. A future in which human workers are replaced by machines is about to become a reality at an insurance firm in Japan, where more than 30 employees are being laid off and replaced with an artificial intelligence system that can calculate payouts to policyholders.

Fukoku Mutual Life Insurance believes it will increase productivity by 30% and see a return on its investment in less than two years. The firm said it would save about 140m yen (£1m) a year after the 200m yen (£1.4m) AI system is installed this month. Maintaining it will cost about 15m yen (£100k) a year. The move is unlikely to be welcomed, however, by 34 employees who will be made redundant by the end of March.

The system is based on IBM's Watson Explorer, which, according to the tech firm, possesses "cognitive technology that can think like a human", enabling it to "analyse and interpret all of your data, including unstructured text, images, audio and video".The technology will be able to read tens of thousands of medical certificates and factor in the length of hospital stays, medical histories and any surgical procedures before calculating payouts, according to the Mainichi Shimbun.

While the use of AI will drastically reduce the time needed to calculate Fukoku Mutual's payouts – which reportedly totalled 132,000 during the current financial year – the sums will not be paid until they have been approved by a member of staff, the newspaper said.

Japan's shrinking, ageing population, coupled with its prowess in robot technology, makes it a prime testing ground for AI. According to a 2015 report by the Nomura Research Institute, nearly half of all jobs in Japan could be performed by robots by 2035. For example, one Japan insurance company, Dai-Ichi Life Insurance has already introduced a Watson-based system to assess payments - although it has not cut staff numbers - and Japan Post Insurance is interested in introducing a similar setup, the Mainichi said. AI could soon be playing a role in the country's politics. Next month, the economy, trade and industry ministry will introduce AI on a trial basis to help civil servants draft answers for ministers during cabinet meetings and parliamentary sessions. The ministry hopes AI will help reduce the punishingly long hours bureaucrats spend preparing written answers for ministers.

● AI public service workers

The automated city: do we still need humans to run public services? If the experiment is a success, it could be adopted by other government agencies, according the Jiji news agency. If, for example a question is asked about energy-saving policies, the AI system will provide civil servants with the relevant data and a list of pertinent debating points based on past answers to similar questions.

The march of Japan's AI robots hasn't been entirely glitch-free, however. At the end of last year a team of researchers abandoned an attempt to develop a robot intelligent enough to pass the entrance exam for the prestigious Tokyo University. "AI is not good at answering the type of questions that require an ability to grasp meanings across a broad spectrum," Noriko Arai, a professor at the National Institute of Informatics, told Kyodo news agency. Hence, AI will have possible to replace some public service workers' tasks.

● AI replace warehouse workers

Denso's use of Drishti shows how some jobs will be transformed by artificial intelligence even when they're unlikely to be eliminated by AI anytime soon. Many jobs in manufacturing require dexterity and resourcefulness, for example, in ways that robots and software still can't match. But advances in AI and sensors are providing new ways to digitize manual labor. That gives managers new insights—and potentially leverage—on workers. For example,some workers say the results are unpleasant. Last year, Amazon warehouse employees in Minnesota staged a walkout to protest how the company uses inventory and worker-tracking technology. They allege that Amazon uses it to enforce a punishing working pace that causes injuries. The company has disputed those claims, saying it coaches employees on how to safely meet quotas.

Workers at Denso were initially wary of the prospect of being video-recorded all day to feed machine-learning algorithms, but Huffman says they have since come to appreciate Drishti's technology. After something goes wrong, workers can now look at the data and video with their managers, instead of having to hope bosses take their account of what happened seriously. Huffman says having a constant readout on productivity also helps managers be more responsive to nascent problems. "If somebody's struggling, not every associate is going to call for help," he says. "If we see their cycle time is jumping through the roof, we can go over and say 'Are you having any issues?'" Workers on Denso lines equipped with Drishti's technology now get a personal feed of their own data. Monitors on each workstation display how a worker is doing, says Raja Shembekar, a Denso vice president. If the worker completes their assembly step on time, they see a smiley face—if not, a frowny one. Hence, Amazon had begun to apply AI robotic to replace some warehouse workers' tasks.

For another factory manufacture working environment example, AI can replace many manufacture workers to do their tasks in factories. Route 9 skims by Boston and cuts clear across Massachusetts to Pittsfield, a city of roughly 50,000, the largest in Berkshire County. Well east of Pittsfield, Route 9 becomes Worcester Road, named for a city that in earlier times was the nation's largest manufacturer of wire—barbed wire, electrical wire, telephone wire and the wire used in the making of undergarments by the Royal Worcester Corset Co., once the largest employer of women in the United States. Older Worcester residents can still recall the factory bells pealing to signal the start and end of the workday. Now, the bells are silent, and the wire and corset factories have been replaced with three of the nation's largest employers: Walmart, Target and Home Depot. If this sounds familiar, it should. It has been nearly two decades since retail overtook manufacturing as the nation's most important job creator, employing roughly one of every 10 American workers—more people than in health care and construction combined. That's a lot of jobs.

Of course, not all retail jobs qualify as what most of us consider good jobs. Today, the average hourly wage for a nonsupervisory retail worker is $11.24, and less than half of retail workers receive benefits of any kind. Still, as a nation, we've come to a sort of uneasy peace with this trend. We know that manufacturing employs far fewer Americans today than it once did—that iPads and Macs aren't made in America and neither are many televisions, appliances, tools, toys or clothes. We also know that shopping for these appliances, tools, toys and clothes is an all-American pastime: On average, we spend nearly 45 minutes a day (more than 270 hours per year) purchasing goods and services. Retail has become the world as we know it, and many of us expect to make our living working in that world.Thanks to automation and a killer business model, Amazon is so efficient that it reaps nearly twice the revenue per employee of Walmart, despite the fact that Walmart, too, has a substantial online presence. Worldwide, Amazon has installed over 100,000 robots to labor in "perfect symbiosis" with humans in its warehouses and has plans to install many thousands more. While it's not clear what constitutes perfect symbiosis, the robots are said to save the company $22 million annually, per warehouse. The company's master plan of an autonomous future also includes goods delivered by drones and self-driving vehicles.

For while Amazon continues to open warehouses around the globe and staff them with many thousands of human beings, estimates are that every human on the Amazon payroll—whether full- or part-time—displaces two humans at traditional brick-and-mortar operations. And that's a feature, not a bug: As Tim Lindner, a veteran IT analyst, confided in a note to industry insiders, eradicating jobs is the explicit goal of any online retailer. As he once wrote: "Labor is the highest-cost factor in warehouse operations. It is no secret that Amazon is moving to highly automated operations within its distribution centers, and...it has additional technology that can further reduce the number of humans it needs to process customer orders.... You have heard the old programmer's phrase, 'Garbage in, garbage out.'... [With] the diminishing reading abilities of humans on the Receiving dock, finding an automated solution to eliminate the 'garbage in' problem is the holy grail. Amazon may have just patented it."

By garbage, Lindner meant human error, the alternative to which is apparently robotic precision. And robots can be very precise, especially when it comes to routine tasks. Sawyer, an industrial robot created by the former Boston-based Rethink Robotics, offers an impressive illustration of how all-embracing a robot arm can be. Sawyer is the brainchild of Rodney Brooks, the inventor of both Roomba, the robotic vacuum, and PackBot, the robot used to clear bunkers in Iraq and Afghanistan and at the World Trade Center after 9/11. Unlike Roomba and PackBot, Sawyer looks almost human—it has an animated flat-screen face and wheels where its legs should be. Simply grabbing and adjusting its monkey-like arm and guiding it through a series of motions "teaches" Sawyer whatever repeatable procedure one needs it to get done. The robot can sense and manipulate objects almost as quickly and as fluidly as a human and demands very little in return: While traditional industrial robots require costly engineers and programmers to write and debug their code, a high school dropout can learn to program Sawyer in less than five minutes. Brooks once estimated that, all told, Sawyer (and his older brother, the two-armed Baxter robot) would work for a "wage" equivalent of less than $4 an hour.

Robots loom large in discussions of work and its future, a conversation that can get mired in false assumptions. Until recently, many economists were skeptical that automation could permanently displace human workers on a large scale. People have always shifted away from work better done by machines, but the economic principle of "comparative advantage" predicts that humans will maintain an edge in many fields. Under this logic, technology will not displace us but set us free to do less dangerous, more challenging things, essentially the very things that make humans human. Of course, human workers are complicated. We get tired, hungry, distracted, angry, confused. We make mistakes, sometimes egregious ones. Machines lack our frailties and biases and are better equipped to weigh evidence fairly, without prejudice or false assumptions. Perhaps most critically, machines can retain and process data far more accurately than we can, and that data is growing exponentially.

Every minute of every day, Google services 3.6 million searches in the United States alone. Spammers send 100 million emails. Snapchatters send 527,000 photos, and the Weather Channel broadcasts 18 million forecasts. This and more data—properly collected, codified and analyzed—can be applied to automate almost any high-order task. Data can also serve as a surrogate for human experience and intuition. Online shopping and social media sites "learn" our preferences and use that information to make values-based assessments to influence our decisions and behavior. And, increasingly, machines excel in the tasks once thought uniquely human."Computers are able to see and hear, and have face-recognition capabilities that are significantly better than humans," says Vardi. "Machines understand the human world far better than they did just a few years ago. And we haven't discovered anything in the human brain that can't be modeled."

● AI can replace counter cashier service staffs

And robots need not be perfect, only equal to—or a tad better than—complicated and expensive humans. And technologists are working hard to make sure they are a tad better. For example, in the case of retail, it's become clear that many of us avoid the self-service checkout line—we prefer the cashier to punch in our purchases rather than do so ourselves. So it seems that the job of cashier—among the largest retail employment categories—is not directly at risk. But Zeynep Ton, an MIT management expert who focuses on the retail sector, says self-service checkout is only a first step and not a terribly smart one. "Customers recognized that self-service checkout is not an innovation, but merely a way of outsourcing the job to them, so they didn't like it," she says. "But new technology is coming that will make self-service checkout so much easier and faster, and that will have a real impact on retail employment."

Experts caution that the so-called apocalypse in retail predicted a few years ago has not yet come to pass. In fact, for every company closing existing stores, two more are opening new stores. Retail is a highly competitive industry, and technology is transforming not only the way we shop but the way we connect with brands—for example, just a few years ago, who would have imagined that Amazon would open actual retail stores? And while e-commerce has grown to 10 percent of retail, that still leaves 90 percent for brick-and-mortar stores. But those brick-and-mortar stores, too, are undergoing radical change that has serious implications for America's workforce.

As example, Lobaugh cites food trucks, which he says increasingly pose a threat to many fast-food outlets. Unlike restaurants pinned down by a pair of Golden Arches, food trucks are nimble—they can home in on areas where customers are most likely to gather at any particular time. They can also tailor their offerings to a particular region or even a neighborhood, as well as use Facebook or other media to get out the word on their menu items and locations. Small, specialty stores also have far more flexibility than large department stores. "Technology has reduced the cost of entry into new markets, so in retail there are fewer big, monolithic companies, but more small competitors," he says. "Companies are diversifying to meet the specific needs and desires of consumers—everyone's piece is getting smaller, but there are many more pieces."

But despite what it predicts will be a banner holiday season, this year Amazon took on far fewer seasonal employees than usual—100,000 employees versus 120,000 the previous two years. And while an Amazon spokeswoman insisted that automation is not a factor in this reduced workforce, others seem to not agree. In a recent report, Morgan Stanley analyst Brian Nowak soothed the fears of Amazon shareholders concerned with the wage increase by pointing out that automation had already and would continue to reduce the call for labor, and therefore reduce overall costs. When asked about this, Lobaugh again tactfully declined to comment—other than to say that while the retail sector had lost less ground than most people assume, retail employees were another matter. "There are winners," he says, "and then there are losers."

- AI can replace accountants in accountancy service industry

Not that long ago artificial intelligence (AI), robots and machine learning (ML) were thought to be things only found in science fiction films. Today, this type of technology is taking center stage in workplaces across the globe. Industries, including manufacturing, retail, agriculture, and customer service have already had AI replace some job positions that left workers scrambling to find new career options. This AI revolution is not expected to slow down anytime soon. In fact, experts anticipate that as many as 800 million jobs could be replaced with AI technology by the year 2030. Initially, AI technology and automation in the workplace seemed to only affect pink and blue-collar workers. As this technology advances and becomes more powerful, professional, white-collar workers, including accountants, are starting to worry about what the future holds for their career and if AI will be developed to own their professional skills in accounting service industry.

In basic terms, AI technology is intelligent machines that are able to complete repetitive, mundane tasks at a fraction of the time it takes humans and with greater accuracy. The emergence of Machine Learning now allows AI platforms to observe, analyze and self-learn data and processes to improve its performance and accuracy over time. AI technology is already able to handle many accounting functions, such as tax preparation, payroll, and audits. Many of the leading accounting software providers, including Xero, Intuit and Sage have incorporated AI technology into their software to handle basic accounting tasks, such as bank reconciliations, invoice categorization, risk assessment, and audit processes, like expense submissions and invoice payments. Many of these standard tasks are extremely time-consuming, which has many accountants across the country worried about how the emerging AI technology will affect their billable hours. An even bigger concern is that AI technologies will replace the need for companies to work with accountants at all.

- AI Will Transform not Replace Accountants

While there is no doubt that AI technology is capable of handling many standard accounting tasks faster and more efficiently or that these capabilities will only increase over time, it doesn't mean the end for accountants. There always will be a need for that human element - human intelligence - at the other end of AI technology. In fact, according to leading research firm, Gartner, AI is set to create more jobs than it will replace, leaving workers, including accountants with options. Accountants don't have to worry about their job being replaced by AI any time in the near future. Companies will always need accountants that can analyze and interpret AI data, as well as provide consulting services. Rather than replacing the role of an accountant, AI technology will transform the duties an accountant performs.

With AI technology and machine learning handling many of the mundane, repetitive tasks, accountants will have more time to focus on other aspects of the job, such as consulting and data analysis. This is good news for many accountants. Rather than spending hours completing menial tasks, accountants of the future will be able to use and analyze AI data to provide their clients with sound business solutions.

In many ways, AI will help accountants improve their services. AI technology will improve data entry accuracy and lower the liability risk for accountants. In addition, emerging technology is more efficient at fraud detection, adding an extra layer of protection for accountants and their clients. It also provides real-time data, which allows accountants to provide real-time solutions. Even more impressive is the ability of machine learning to analyze large amounts of data instantly, evaluate past successes and failures in an effort to accurately predict future outcomes.

There is no way to escape the use of AI technology, at least not if you hope to remain competitive in the upcoming years. The speed, efficiency and accuracy of AI technology just cannot be beat. The only thing accountants can do is to embrace this new technology and learn how to maximize its use. The better equipped you are to help your clients integrate and utilize AI technology in their accounting processes the more valuable you will be. For example, many universities today are already incorporating IT and database management courses into their accounting program. This means that graduating students are coming into the workforce with the skills they need for future accounting work. Accountants already in the workforce must find ways to acquire these skills in order to remain relevant to their employers and/or their clients. Accountants can obtain the IT skills they need by attending seminars, using self-learning online programs or attending college-level courses. It is equally important for accountants to stay up-to-date on the latest accounting trends, emerging technologies and industry news. This will allows accountants to not only keep their jobs but to also provide more efficient services to their clients. Rather than worry about AI taking over their jobs, accountants should embrace this technology as a powerful solution to enhance customer services. Finally, accountants will be able to use all their training and experience to provide customer will real and effective business solutions, whether it's in reference to tax consulting, real estate deals, mergers, growth options, or any other business practice.

On conclusion, technology is advancing at record rates so now is the time to obtain the IT and database management skills you need to advance into the future. With the right skills and training, accountants are guaranteed a lucrative career that will last well into the future.

Why Developed And Developing Countries Need Artificial Intelligent Development To Assist Office Tasks

Must developed and developing countries need artificial intelligent development to assist office tasks ? Ought AI is needed to prefer to develop technique to assist office staffs to reduce workload to compare other kinds of occupation environment tasks aspects ? If one developed country, e.g. US, UK , Japan , Singapore it does not continue to develop artificial intelligence, robotic, then what disadvantges or weaknesses , it will encounter to compare when it chooses to continue to develop this artificial intelligent technology in society. If one developing country, e.g. China, Korea, Taiwan, it does not continue to develop artificial intelligence, robotic, then what disadantages or weaknesses, it will also encounter to compare when it chooses to continue to develop this artificial intelligent technology in in society. I shall explan the reasons why the results may cause to either the developed country, or the developing country as below:

● How AI help developing countries to communication and agriculture and learning and medical delivery development

Why can AI help developing countries ? Drones that pick inaccessible crops and mobile phones that give medical advice are two of the ways AI can transform life in the developing world. Artificial intelligence (AI) may improve the lives of the world's poor, the technology needed to revolutionise inefficient, ineffective food and healthcare systems in developing countries is well. For example, in low-income areas, agriculture and healthcare are two critical ecosystems that we can apply AI to immediately; this is not the far future, or even in five years.

Artificial intelligence (AI) has seeped into the daily lives of people in the developed world. From virtual assistants to recommendation engines, AI is in the news, our homes and offices. There is a lot of potential in terms of AI usage, especially in humanitarian areas. The impact could have a multiplier effect in developing countries, where resources are limited.

Emergency Response to developing countries' earthquake natural damage suddence occurrence predicting

AI and machine learning are still finding importance in emerging markets, but certain applications have emerged and are now widely used. For instance, predictive models for disaster relief enable first responders to automatically analyze large-scale behavior and movement through multiple sources of data including social media platforms, web forums, news sources, etc. Based on collected data, responders can scale reconstruction efforts and distribute supplies in a timely manner.

Why and how AI can assist farmers to predict when the earthquake occurs suddenly in order to avoid or reduce the natural damage to their agriculture productive number loss. For example, In 2015, when a major earthquake hit Nepal, more than 8 million people were affected. During the aftermath, drones were used to map and assess the destruction and speed up the rescue mission. The town of Sankhu, situated about 20 kilometers northeast of Kathmandu, was among the highly affected locations. In May 2018, my company Fusemachines and GeoSpatial Systems partnered with Sankhu's city officials to use drones and artificial intelligence in an effort to automatically estimate the reconstruction need. After processing data accumulated from a drone-powered aerial mapping of the region, the team fed this data to advanced machine learning algorithms. Combining drone imagery, digital mapping and machine learning, the team configured region modeling and infrastructure development with higher accuracy. Another organization known as One Concern, a California-based startup, has created a predictive AI program called Seismic Concern to accurately predict seism and is also working on solutions for wildfires, floods and hurricanes.

Smart AI Agriculture

Another application of AI in developing countries is smart agriculture. Farmers monitor crops more effectively and make better predictions on planting, weeding and harvesting using AI tools. It can also be used to analyze one plant at a time and add pesticides only to infected plants and trees instead of spraying pesticides across large swaths of crops. One California-based tech company is an example of this use of AI. So, the developing countries farmers in rural parts of India are also using AI to increase yields through better access to information about the farming season than they would normally have. Technology-enabled process automation offers the agribusiness industry the chance for remarkable growth -- not only in developed countries but around the world. There's a unique opportunity to increase yields, cut down labor costs and improve people's health.

Medicine Delivery to developing countries' patients urgent need

Companies are also leveraging AI to improve access to health care in some of the most remote areas of the world. In Rwanda, for example, Zipline is using drones to deliver medical supplies and blood to hospitals and clinics that are difficult to access by car. This has dramatically impacted people living in remote parts of the country because they are able to get medical help when needed. The drone system in Rwanda has also helped reduce waste of blood by 95%, as noted by Zipline. One Concern has created an AI program called Seismic Concern that accurately predicts seismic events and is also working on solutions for floods, wildfires and hurricanes. The medical field may actually benefit the most from emerging technologies in developing countries.

Assistance to reduce teaching work workload or psychological pressure to teachers in developing countries' schools

Another vital area benefiting from innovative technologies like AI is education. Advanced technologies can enhance how we learn, teach and perform tasks. In most developing countries, schools lack experienced teachers and resources to enhance students' knowledge. As a result, many students still have to walk long distances to get to the nearest school, which has created education gaps, especially in rural areas. AI tools such as personalized learning assistants can simplify learning by making tutoring services and learning materials accessible to all students, wherever they are. Machines can be automated to help students learn basic concepts without a tutor, which companies like Carnegie Learning are working on. This would allow students to learn at any time from anywhere. With AI, education is made easy and accessible to more people.

The initial usage of AI in developing countries has been at a micro level -- solving small, specific problems in a defined industry. As machine learning advances and there is a higher utilization of AI, we will see more complex issues being targeted and resolved. When duly adopted, AI can positively impact future developing countries people everyday lives not just in disaster intervention, education, health care and agriculture but can also help in mitigating poverty, malnutrition and pollution. Especially, in developing nations, to leverage AI's true potential and create a snowball effect. Startups are defining a holistic and humanitarian approach to building more sophisticated, AI-ready societies. Stakeholders in the AI landscape should understand the strengths and nuances of the developing world as well as the limitations of AI and create localized solutions and applications.

Why does smart phone help developing countries communication ?

Internet Seen as Positive Influence on Education but Negative on Morality in Emerging and Developing Nations. Internet access differs substantially across the 32 emerging and developing countries polled, with the lowest rates of internet use in South Asian and sub-Saharan African nations. Within countries, computer owners, young people, the well-educated, the wealthy and those with English language ability are much more likely to access the internet than their counterparts. To access the internet, people increasingly use smartphones rather than more cumbersome fixed landline connections and computers. Around the world, both smartphones and basic-feature phones alike are used for sending messages and taking pictures.

In fact, many developing countries young people, students are popular to use smart phones for internet usage aim, instead of communication. Moreover, many developing countries working people are also popular to use smart phones for any working usage in their working time , even non working time any time. So, smart phones (AI) phones will be important communication or leisure tools to developing countries people in the future. Unless, it is one day, scientists can develop another new communication tool to replace smart phones. So, artificial intelligence will be important to influence developing countries people , how to improve or bring positive learning attitudes to students in their daily learnnng lifes. as well as how to raise developing countries people, how to raise working people efficiency or improve performace in their daily working lifes. So, AI may bring positive learning or working attitudes to developing countries working people and students both.

The Positive Impact of Mass Media in Developing Countries

Radio, newspapers, television, Internet, social media, etc., all of these are forms of mass media. Each of these outlets has the capability of bringing information to thousands of people with one device. While in some communities it is easy to take advantage of these communication outlets such as television and Internet access, not everyone has access to such outlets. Radio is one of the most common forms of mass media in developing countries because it's affordable and uses less electricity than many other forms of mass media, but only approximately 75 percent of people in developing countries have access to a radio, and roughly 77 percent of people in rural areas have access to electricity.

For developing countries that have implemented forms of mass media in their communities, there have been numerous positive outcomes are influenced to impact developing countries mass media by artificial intelligence as below:

When AI is participated to developing countries mass media, it can influence any radio, television audiences raise more attention to each other through social media platforms such as Facebook and Twitter and create, organize and initiate street protests and campaigns. Furthermore, having access to social media in developing countries, people are able to connect to those that they usually wouldn't have the chance to talk to. Moreover, AI Provides educational opportunities- In many countries, the division between local and national languages as well as issues of literacy can make communication difficult. With the use of mass media, a bridge can be built between these two gaps. In India, there is a radio station that provides information in local languages and respects local culture and traditions. One of the main ways is to create public awareness of what is going on with businesses and government officials. The media plays an important role in giving people the opportunity to act against injustice, oppression and misdeeds that they otherwise wouldn't know about. Information on available healthcare, a mass radio broadcast was sent out encouraging parents to seek treatment at local healthcare facilities for their sick children. With this mass outreach on healthcare, the encouragement of people to take their children to healthcare facilities saved thousands of lives. This easy way of encouraging others and bringing awareness about certain diseases was made possible through a simple radio broadcast. Finally, when AI is particiapted to media, it may bring many social issues to life that otherwise would remain unknown to many people. In developing countries and communities like Burkina Faso, when the radio broadcast was released about malaria, diarrhea and pneumonia, people were educated and moved to action and knew to take their children to healthcare facilities for preventative care. As it is seen, having access to different media outlets is vital for those in developing countries. Here are three ways that those in developing countries can implement mass media to help their people and communities.

When AI is participated to any internet radio or internet newspaper mass online listening or reading channel. It can provide online radios or newspapers in public places- By providing online radios and newspapers in public areas it gives community members to access news, information and emergency warnings. Even though radios can be on the cheaper side, there are still many people that can't afford to have a radio in their home. By providing one in a local place, not only would it better educate the community members but also it will bring the community together. So, it can make media outlets a two-way platform- Creating a two-way platform between the community and those who are behind the radio stations, newspapers or broadcasts makes the community feel involved and that their voices are being heard. An organization called Soul City in sub-Saharan Africa is showing how well two-way platforms work by engaging their listeners and having them contribute thoughts and ideas about complex issues. Because developing countries radio listening audiences or newspaper readers are popular to accept computer online radio listening channel or online newspaper reading channel to replace traditional paper newspapers or radio machines. So, AI may raise their listening news or reading news leisure feeling from online mass media channel in the future.

● Why do developed countries need to develop AI

Artificial intelligence, or AI, is driving massive shifts across the globe, and every day more questions arise. What impact will AI have on the workforce and how can we prepare for it? How can we encourage economy-boosting and job-creating technologies? How can we ensure that AI will be implemented ethically and with minimal bias? How will society benefit?

For developed country, such as US example. None of the US, Israel and Russia have a formal national AI policy yet. Private sector companies such as Google, Amazon and Apple and the US department of defence are driving the bulk of AI investment in the United States. Though Israel does not have a specific policy, it is keenly focused on AI and has seen the number of AI start-ups triple since 2014.

Developed country may learn whether what weakness it is lacking when it does not continue to develop AI from one another developed country. Which countries are approaching AI most effectively, and to what degree is there opportunity for greater international collaboration? It may be too early to tell; however, when analyzing the best practices of existing national AI policies, there is much that can be learned. These are the specific areas to consider. When one developed country continue to develop or research AI, it may bring these benefits as below:

On gathering Data aspect, from self-driving vehicles to smart cities, data is the driver behind AI. Innovation in the United States is limited without a national strategy that answers questions about protocol and ownership. France and Denmark, on the other hand, are opening government data. France is hosting troves of centrally collected public and private data that it plans to make available as part of its strategy. Conversely, by taking a restrictive position on issues of data collection (as indicated by the implementation of General Data Protection Regulation), the EU is putting manufacturers and software designers at a disadvantage while balancing the demand for privacy. On raising technologica talent aspect, the demand for AI talent far outweighs the available supply. As a result, almost every nation's strategy addresses talent development. Canada's AI strategy is distinct in that it primarily focuses on research and talent strategy. The country boasts AI degree programmes and is building a $127 million research facility in Toronto. Companies like Facebook and my own company, Uptake, are investing in Canada to access this talent pool. On AI legal technological innovation aspect, a whole host of legal questions swirl around AI. The country is developing a bill for AI liability that will be ready in March 2019. The government hopes the legal framework will attract investors by providing a simple, comprehensive guideline to enable the broad use of AI systems. So, when the developed country applied AI technology to assist any lawyers to work, then AI can help them to reduce the workload to draft any legal documents more easier. So, any developed countries lawyers' draft legal documents time must reduce if the developed countries lawyers accept to apply AI to assist their legal works. One of the great promises of AI is its potential for improving quality of life. But without the right planning and oversight, we risk exacerbating problems of inequality or marginalizing groups of people. As an example, India's AI strategy is focused on leveraging the technology not only for economic growth, but also for social inclusion.

AI may bring what benefits to developed countries

From SIRI to self-driving cars, artificial intelligence (AI) is progressing rapidly. While science fiction often portrays AI as robots with human-like characteristics, AI can encompass anything from Google's search algorithms to IBM's Watson to autonomous weapons. Artificial intelligence today is properly known as narrow AI (or weak AI), in that it is designed to perform a narrow task (e.g. only facial recognition or only internet searches or only driving a car). However, the long-term goal of many researchers is to create general AI (AGI or strong AI). While narrow AI may outperform humans at whatever its specific task is, like playing chess or solving equations, AGI would outperform humans at nearly every cognitive task.

Why research AI safety? Would AI bring war when AI is continued to develop by developed countries? In the near term, the goal of keeping AI's impact on society beneficial motivates research in many areas, from economics and law to technical topics such as verification, validity, security and control. Whereas it may be little more than a minor nuisance if your laptop crashes or gets hacked, it becomes all the more important that an AI system does what you want it to do if it controls your car, your airplane, your pacemaker, your automated trading system or your power grid. Another short-term challenge is preventing a devastating arms race in lethal autonomous weapons.

In the long term, an important question is what will happen if the quest for strong AI succeeds and an AI system becomes better than humans at all cognitive tasks. As pointed out by I.J. Good in 1965, designing smarter AI systems is itself a cognitive task. Such a system could potentially undergo recursive self-improvement, triggering an intelligence explosion leaving human intellect far behind. By inventing revolutionary new technologies, such a superintelligence might help us eradicate war, disease, and poverty, and so the creation of strong AI might be the biggest event in human history. Some experts have expressed concern, though, that it might also be the last, unless we learn to align the goals of the AI with ours before it becomes superintelligent.

There are some who question whether strong AI will ever be achieved, and others who insist that the creation of superintelligent AI is guaranteed to be beneficial. At FLI we recognize both of these possibilities, but also recognize the potential for an artificial intelligence system to intentionally or unintentionally cause great harm. We believe research today will help us better prepare for and prevent such potentially negative consequences in the future, thus enjoying the benefits of AI while avoiding pitfalls.

How can AI be dangerous when developed countries continue to develop AI to become weapon to replace soldiers?

Most researchers agree that a superintelligent AI is unlikely to exhibit human emotions like love or hate, and that there is no reason to expect AI to become intentionally benevolent or malevolent. Instead, when considering how AI might become a risk, experts think two scenarios most likely:

The AI is programmed to do something devastating: Autonomous weapons are artificial intelligence systems that are programmed to kill. In the hands of the wrong person, these weapons could easily cause mass casualties. Moreover, an AI arms race could inadvertently lead to an AI war that also results in mass casualties. To avoid being thwarted by the enemy, these weapons would be designed to be extremely difficult to simply "turn off," so humans could plausibly lose control of such a situation. This risk is one that's present even with narrow AI, but grows as levels of AI intelligence and autonomy increase.

The AI is programmed to do something beneficial, but it develops a destructive method for achieving its goal: This can happen whenever we fail to fully align the AI's goals with ours, which is strikingly difficult. If you ask an obedient intelligent car to take you to the airport as fast as possible, it might get you there chased by helicopters and covered in vomit, doing not what you wanted but literally what you asked for. If a superintelligent system is tasked with a ambitious geoengineering project, it might wreak havoc with our ecosystem as a side effect, and view human attempts to stop it as a threat to be met. So, a super-intelligent AI will be extremely good at accomplishing its goals, and if those goals aren't aligned with ours, we have a problem. You're probably not an evil ant-hater who steps on ants out of malice, but if you're in charge of a hydroelectric green energy project and there's an anthill in the region to be flooded, too bad for the ants. A key goal of AI safety research is to never place humanity in the position of those ants.

Why the recent interest in AI safety ?

Stephen Hawking, Elon Musk, Steve Wozniak, Bill Gates, and many other big names in science and technology have recently expressed concern in the media and via open letters about the risks posed by AI, joined by many leading AI researchers. The idea that the quest for strong AI would ultimately succeed was long thought of as science fiction, centuries or more away. However, thanks to recent breakthroughs, many AI milestones, which experts viewed as decades away merely five years ago, have now been reached, making many experts take seriously the possibility of superintelligence in our lifetime. While some experts still guess that human-level AI is centuries away, most AI researches at the 2015 Puerto Rico Conference guessed that it would happen before 2060. Since it may take decades to complete the required safety research, it is prudent to start it now.

Because AI has the potential to become more intelligent than any human, we have no surprise way of predicting how it will behave. We can't use past technological developments as much of a basis because we've never created anything that has the ability to, wittingly or unwittingly, outsmart us. The best example of what we could face may be our own evolution. People now control the planet, not because we're the strongest, fastest or biggest, but because we're the smartest. If we're no longer the smartest, are we assured to remain in control?

A captivating conversation is taking place about the future of artificial intelligence and what it will/should mean for humanity. There are fascinating controversies where the world's leading experts disagree, such as: AI's future impact on the job market; if/when human-level AI will be developed; whether this will lead to an intelligence explosion; and whether this is something we should welcome or fear. But there are also many examples of of boring pseudo-controversies caused by people misunderstanding and talking past each other. When one developed country continue to develop AI, can itself country's all factories workers will lose jobs, due to AI can replace them to do simple works in factories, or any public transport drivers, e.g. bus drivers, ferry , tram, train drivers, they will lose jobs, when AI (non manual driving drivers) can replace all public transport drivers. So, some occupations will lose if developed countries continue to develop or research AI to replace human to do some simple jobs, such as some cooking jobs can be done by AI. So, it is possible that future cookers won't be needed, because AI cooking skills may be better than them to cook any good taste chinese or western food in restaurants.

If you drive down the road, you have a subjective experience of colors, sounds, etc. But does a self-driving car have a subjective experience? Does it feel like anything at all to be a self-driving car? Although this mystery of consciousness is interesting in its own right, it's irrelevant to AI risk. If you get struck by a driverless car, it makes no difference to you whether it subjectively feels conscious. In the same way, what will affect us humans is what superintelligent AI does, not how it subjectively feels.

In fact, AI may be make any brokers jobs in financial market. the main concern of the beneficial-AI movement isn't with robots but with intelligence itself: specifically, intelligence whose goals are misaligned with ours. To cause us trouble, such misaligned superhuman intelligence needs no robotic body, merely an internet connection – this may enable outsmarting financial markets, out-inventing human researchers, out-manipulating human leaders, and developing weapons we cannot even understand. Even if building robots were physically impossible, a super-intelligent and super-wealthy AI could easily pay or manipulate many humans to unwittingly do its bidding. So, future brokers will be replaced by AI, when AI can be made to own financial brokers' analytical mind to make more accurate whether the share price will rise up or fall down to compare human financial brokers' analytical mind. The robot misconception is related to the myth that machines can't control humans. Intelligence enables control: humans control tigers not because we are stronger, but because we are smarter. This means that if we cede our position as smartest on our planet, it's possible that we might also cede control.

Not wasting time on the above-mentioned misconceptions lets us focus on true and interesting controversies where even the experts disagree. What sort of future do you want? Should we develop lethal autonomous weapons? What would you like to happen with job automation? What career advice would you give today's kids? Do you prefer new jobs replacing the old ones, or a jobless society where everyone enjoys a life of leisure and machine-produced wealth? Further down the road, would you like us to create superintelligent life and spread it through our cosmos? Will we control intelligent machines or will they control us? Will intelligent machines replace us, coexist with us, or merge with us? What will it mean to be human in the age of artificial intelligence?

Why do developed countries people need AI ?

Why do we assume that AI will require more and more physical space and more power when human intelligence continuously manages to miniaturize and reduce power consumption of its devices. How low the power needs and how small will the machines be by the time quantum computing becomes reality? Why do we assume that AI will exist as independent machines? If so, and the AI is able to improve its Intelligence by reprogramming itself, will machines driven by slower processors feel threatened, not by mere stupid humans, but by machines with faster processors? What would drive machines to reproduce themselves when there is no biological incentive, pressure or need to do so?

Who says superior AI will need or want to have a physical existence when an immaterial AI could evolve and preserve itself better from external dangers. What will happen if AI developed by competing ideologies, liberalism vs communism, reach maturity at the same time, will they fight for hegemony by trying to destroy each other physically and/or virtually. If AI is programmed to believe in God, and competing AI emerges programmed by muslims, christians or jews, how are the different AI's going to make sense of the different religious beliefs, are we going to have AI religious wars? What if the "powers that be" greatest fear is the emergence of a super AI that police's and rationalizes the distribution of wealth and food. A friendly super AI that is programmed to help humanity by, enforcing the declaration of Human Rights (the US is the only industrialized country that to this day has not signed this declaration) ending corruption and racism and protecting the environment.Most benefits of civilization stem from intelligence, so how can we enhance these benefits with artificial intelligence without being replaced on the job market and perhaps altogether?

Key to the process of machine learning are neural networks. These are brain-inspired networks of interconnected layers of algorithms, called neurons, that feed data into each other, and which can be trained to carry out specific tasks by modifying the importance attributed to input data as it passes between the layers. During training of these neural networks, the weights attached to different inputs will continue to be varied until the output from the neural network is very close to what is desired, at which point the network will have 'learned' how to carry out a particular task. A subset of machine learning is deep learning, where neural networks are expanded into sprawling networks with a huge number of layers that are trained using massive amounts of data. It is these deep neural networks that have fuelled the current leap forward in the ability of computers to carry out task like speech recognition and computer vision.

In conclusion, when developed countries continue to develop AI, it may bring positive advantages to bring raising productivies, or efficiencies, but it may also raise unemployment ratio to any low skill or low knowledge jobs in ther societies. However, human future society will need to change to be better to raise our living standard. But AI is one kind the best choice tool to achieve this aim in our future, so I agree developed countries continue to develop or research AI to be the super -human machine.

Artificial Intelligence Worker Brings

Working Environment Influences

Robots were once known only for the manufacturing business but today they are very much part of many workplaces. The future is even more promising for this wonder of artificial intelligence.Imagine a robot doing some of the major tasks of managers like using data to evaluate problems, making better decisions, monitoring team performance, and even setting goals.

Technology is playing a pivotal role in helping humans work more effectively. Since automation has become an integral part of business operations, we can predict that robots are soon going to replace many jobs that are today performed by humans. Now that the corporate world is also on the cusp of entering the robotic age, let's see what pros and cons this technology offers business world. If one day, our global working environments have any kinds of robotic participates to our service and warehouse and office etc. different working environment in order to assist office workers, service workers, warehouse workers, professional lawyers, doctors accountants job duties, what positive or negative influences, it will bring to what negative or positive effects to any office , warehouse, shopping centre, hospital, transport , restaurant etc, different working environments. Can robotic help office , warehouse to raise efficency ? Can robotic help hospital, restaurant, cinema, shopping center to improve service performance? Can robotic influence working environment to be worse? Can robotic help office or any working places to reduce expenditure or reduce long time machine and salary cost when they do not need more employees or machines , due to robotic workers assistance.

I shall attempt to explain whether robotic workers will bring what positive or negative influence to our future working environment as below:

Advantages to robotic bring to working environment

What advantages thar robotic will bring to working environment? They may include: Many people fear that robots or full automation may someday take their jobs, but this is simply not the case. Robots bring more advantages than disadvantages to the workplace. They enrich a company's ability to succeed while improving the lives of real, human employees who are still needed to keep operations running smoothly. If you're thinking about investing in some robots, share the advantages with your employees. You might be surprised at how many of them are quick to support the idea.

1. Safety

Safety is the most obvious advantage of utilizing robotics. Heavy machinery, machinery that runs at hot temperature, and sharp objects can easily injure a human being. By delegating dangerous tasks to a robot, you're more likely to look at a repair bill than a serious medical bill or a lawsuit. Employees who work dangerous jobs will be thankful that robots can remove some of the risks.

2. Speed

Robots don't get distracted or need to take breaks. They don't request vacation time or ask to leave an hour early. A robot will never feel stressed out and start running slower. They also don't need to be invited to employee meetings or training session. Robots can work all the time, and this speeds up production. They keep your employees from having to overwork themselves to meet high pressure deadlines or seemingly impossible standards.

3. Consistency

Robots never need to divide their attention between a multitude of things. Their work is never contingent on the work of other people. They won't have unexpected emergencies, and they won't need to be relocated to complete a different time sensitive task. They're always there, and they're doing what they're supposed to do. Automation is typically far more reliable than human labor.

4. Perfection

Robots will always deliver quality. Since they're programmed for precise, repetitive motion, they're less likely to make mistakes. In some ways, robots are simultaneously an employee and a quality control system. A lack of quirks and preferences, combined with the eliminated possibility of human error, will create a predictably perfect product every time.

5. Happier Employees

Since robots are often assigned to perform tasks that people don't particularly enjoy, like menial work, repetitive motion, or dangerous jobs, your employees are more likely to be happy. They'll be focusing on more engaging work that's less likely to grind down their nerves. They might want to take advantage of additional educational opportunities, utilize your employee wellness program, or participate in an innovative workplace project. They'll be happy to let the robots do the work that leaves them feeling burned out.

6. Job Creation

Robots don't take jobs away. They merely change the jobs that exist. Robots need people for monitoring and supervision. The more robots we need, the more people we'll need to build those robots. By training your employees to work with robots, you're giving them a reason to stay motivated in their position with your company. They'll be there for the advancements and they'll have the unique opportunity to develop a new set of tech or engineering related skills.

7. Productivity

Robots can't do everything. Some jobs absolutely need to be completed by a human. If your human employees aren't caught up doing the things that could have easily be left for robots, they'll be available and productive. They can talk to customers, answer emails and social media comments, help with branding and marketing, and sell products. You'll be amazed at how much they can accomplish when the grunt work isn't weighing them down.

8. Cost reduce

The first and the foremost advantage of having robots in workplaces is their cost. Robots are much cheaper than humans and their cost is now decreasing. It's a fact that we cannot compare human abilities with robots but robotic capabilities are now growing quickly. For example, if you run an essay writing service, you can use robots to perform every kind of research related to any subject. Because robots are more active and don't get tired like humans, the collaboration between humans and robots is reducing absenteeism. The pace of human cannot increase hence robots are helping humans.

However,robots are more precise than humans; they don't tremble or shake as human hands. Robots have smaller and versatile moving parts which help them in performing tasks with more accuracy than humans. There is no doubt that robots are significantly stronger and faster than humans. Robots come in any shape and size, depending upon the need of the task. Robots can work anywhere in any environmental condition whether it is space, underwater, in extreme heat or wind etc. Robots can be used everywhere where human safety is a huge concern. Robots are programmed by a human;

they cannot say no to anything and can be used for any dangerous and unwanted work where humans may deny to offer their services. For example, many robotic probes have been sent into space but have never returned. Robots in warfare are saving more lives and have now proven to be very successful. For example, in chemical factory environment, robots are now being used in the chemical industry and can, for example deal with chemical spills in a nuclear plant, which would otherwise pose a major health concern. Cost-effectiveness is one of the most sound arguments to be made for the case of industrial robots. Robots will reduce production costs by eliminating internal costs to compensate human salaries. Businesses are forecasting that their profitability will increase once they implement robots into production, or that they will have more financial mobility to invest in new products or technologies.

9. productive efficiency

Quality assurance is expected with the use of machinery in production. Industrial robots will be able to ensure consistency with mass production of manufactured products. The possible human error that assembly line workers pose the threat of will be removed. Optimized production efficiency means that a general manager will be able to have set quantity and quality standards that will be met by robots. Production quotas will not be jeopardized by low concentration, break time and employee injuries, among other things. The efficiency of production forecasts and supply levels will be increased with robots, able to be programmed to work at the optimal speed for a given plant. Limiting human work in hazardous environments, because manufacturing jobs often place workers at more physical risk compared to a lot of other industries. Lowering the level of a hazard presented to employees on the job is attractive to executives to preserve company reputation and minimize potential legal liabilities.

10. Reducing longer working hours

Typically people have to have breaks, get distracted and after time attention drops and pace slows. With a robot it can work 24/7, and keeps running at 100%. Typically if you replace one person on a key process in a production line with a robot the output increases by 40% in the same working hours just because a robot has more stamina and never stops. Robots also don't take holidays or have unexpected days off sick.

11. Increased profitability

By increasing the efficiency of your production process, reducing the resource and time needed to complete it, and also achieving higher quality products, industrial robots can thus be used to achieve higher profitability levels overall, with lower cost per product.

12. Improved working environment

Industrial robots are often used for performing tasks which are deemed as dangerous for humans, as well as being able to perform highly laborious and repetitive tasks. Overall, by using industrial robots you can improve the working conditions and safety in your factory or production process. Robots don't get tired and make dangerous mistakes, neither do they suffer from repetitive strain injury.Due to their high accuracy levels, robots can also be used to produce higher quality products which adhere to certain standards of quality, whilst also reducing the time needed for quality control.Industrial robots are able to complete certain tasks faster and better than people, as they are designed to perform these tasks with a higher accuracy level. This and the fact that they are used to automate processes which previously might have taken significantly more time and resources, means that you can often use industrial robots to increase the efficiency of your production line.

13. Improved Quality Assurance

Few workers enjoy doing repetitive tasks and after a certain period of time concentration levels will naturally decline. This lapse in concentration is known as vigilance decrement and can often lead to costly errors for the business and sometimes serious injury to the member of staff.Robotic automation eliminates these risks by accurately producing and checking items meet the required standard without fail. With more product going out the door manufactured to a higher standard, this creates a number of new business possibilities for companies to expand upon.

14. Increased Productivity

Using robotic automation to tackle repetitive tasks makes complete sense. Robots are designed to make repetitive movements. Humans, also by design, are not. The introduction of automation into your manufacturing process has many different productivity benefits, some of which are shown here.Giving staff members the opportunity to expand on their skills and work in other areas will create a better environment which the business as a whole will benefit from. With higher energy levels and more focus put into their work, the product can only improve, which will also lead to extremely satisfied clients.

15. Avoiding workers need to work In Hazardous Environments
Aside from potential injuries in the workplace, staff members in particular industries can be asked to work in unstable or dangerous environments. For example, if a high level of chemicals are present, robotic automation offers the ideal solution, as it will continue to work without harm. Production areas that require extremely high or low temperatures typically have a high turnover of staff due to the nature of the work. Automated robots can minimise material waste and remove the need for humans to put themselves at unnecessary risk.

Disadvantages to robotic bring to working environment
1. Increase unemployment rate and job loss
On working environment cost increasing aspect, where robots are increasing the efficiency in many businesses, they are also increasing the unemployment rate. Because of robots, human labour is no longer required in many factories and manufacturing plants. They can certainly handle their prescribed tasks, but they typically cannot handle unexpected situations.The ROI of your business may suffer if your operation relies on too many robots. They have higher expenses than humans, so at the end of the day you may not always achieve the desired ROI.
However, robots may have AI but they are certainly not as intelligent as humans. They can never improve their jobs outside the pre-defined programming because they simply cannot think for themselves. Robots installed in workplaces still require manual labour attached to them. Training those employees on how to work with the robots definitely has a cost attached to it.Moreover, robots have no sense of emotions or conscience. They lack empathy and this is one major disadvantage of having an emotionless workplace.Also, robots operate on the basis of information fed to them through a chip. If one thing goes wrong the entire company bears the loss. Where a robot saves times, on the other hand it can also result in a lag. It is, after all, a machine so you cannot expect too much from them. If a robot malfunctions, you need extra time to fix it, which would require reprogramming.If ultimately robots would do all the work, and the humans will just sit and monitor them, health hazards will increase rapidly. Obesity will be on top of the list. So there are advantages, but there are disadvantages as well. It is the twenty first century and we cannot work without machines.Humans are still considered far more efficient than robots when it comes to decision making powers, handling difficult situations, brainstorming, and generally bringing a sense of emotion and

empathy into a workplace. Besides, you cannot rule out the significant role of humans in a business. After all, no machine can replace the human factor 'real employees' bring into a workplace. So, AI can raise unemployment and increase factory or shopping center or office working environment cost when their working environment are applied robotic to replace many workers, then machine electricity expense will also increase. Otherwise, human workers can not spend too much electricity expense in cost aspect.
Whilst industrial robots can prove highly effective and bring you a positive ROI, implementing them might require a fairly high capital cost. That's why, before making a decision we recommend considering both the investment needed and also the ROI you expect to achieve. Often the easiest way to get round this issue is to take out asset finance and the ROI of the robot more than pays for the interest on the asset finance.
This is typically the biggest obstacle that will decide whether or not a company will invest in robotic automation, or wait until a later stage. A comprehensive business case must be built when considering the implementation of this technology. The returns can be substantial and quite often occur within a short space of time. However, the cash flow must be sustainable in the meantime and the stability of the company is by no means worth the risk if the returns are only marginal. Yet, in most instances there will be a repayment schedule available, which makes it a lot easier to afford and control finances. Our downloadable automation payback calculator also has a finance scheme option so you can see how this would work for you.
On job loss increasing aspect, Job loss is by far the most significant opposition frequently brought against the use of robots in the manufacturing industry. Industry workers of all levels, from entry-level to veterans, worry about the security of their employment status, and the ability of their job to be replaced by a robot. This panic is more widespread in this industry compared to others because of the closer immanence of a robot takeover in manufacturing.
Macro effects are another topic that usually comes up with job loss. More "big picture" thinkers wonder how the national, and eventually global economy will be affected when manufacturing workers' jobs are displaced. How can this mass unemployment possibly be compensated for, and how can the robots' presumed success be limited from seeping into other industries. However, increased investment costs are a financial counterpoint to industrial robots, with the idea that manufacturing companies will rack up their debt investing in robotic technology. Firms

that do not have the funding might even go bankrupt in an effort to keep up with industry trends rather than continue on with normalized operations.Hence, elimination of a whole labor class would presumably occur a bit of a ways down the road, but the implications of this point are too large not to consider. Bringing in robots to take unskilled labor jobs will place more pressure on the economy, education system, and financial market, just to name a few. The United States has always been associated with the grit and work ethic of its blue-collar workers, and robots are threatening to eliminate this aspect of the human population, with a take over of production jobs.

One of the biggest concerns surrounding the introduction of robotic automation is the impact of jobs for workers. If a robot can perform at a faster, more consistent rate, then the fear is that humans may not be needed at all. While these worries are understandable, they are not really accurate.The same was said during the early years of the industrial revolution, and as history has showed us, humans continued to play an essential role. Amazon are a great example of this. The employment rate has grown rapidly during a period where they have gone from using around 1,000 robots to over 45,000

2. Robotic can not perform better to compare human workers, when they need to work long time in any working environment

Robots need a supply of power, The people can lose jobs in factories, They need maintenance to keep them running, It costs a lot of money to make or buy robots, The software and the equipment that you need to use with the robot cost much money. Robots cost much money in maintenance & repair, The programs need to be updated to suit the changing requirements, the machines need to be made smarter, In case of breakdown, the cost of repair may be very high, The procedures to restore lost code or data may be time-consuming & costly.

Robots can store large amounts of data but the storage, access, retrieval is not as effective as the human brain, They can perform repetitive tasks for a long time but they do not get better with experience such as the humans do. Robots are not able to act any different from what they are programmed to do, With the heavy application of robots, the humans may become overly dependent on the machines, losing their mental capacities, If the control of robots goes in the wrong hands, Robots may cause the destruction. Robots are not intelligent or sentient, They can never improve the results of their jobs outside of their predefined programming, They do not think, They do not have emotions or conscience, This limits how the robots can help & interact with people. Robots can take the place of many humans in factories, So, the people have to find new jobs or be retrained, They can take the place of the humans in several situations, If the robots begin to replace the humans in every field, They will lead to unemployment.

Humans fear robots, Robots inspire two types of fear: firstly, that they might take over our jobs, and secondly, that they could take over the world, Robots will steal our jobs, Robots have the effect of increasing productivity rather than eliminating jobs.Robotics become increasingly present in our everyday life, with household robots, medical, industrial, on production lines, not to mention airports, banks, and hotels, So, Robots may dominate the human species. Robots can operate on the basis of information fed to them through a chip, when one thing goes wrong the entire company bears a loss.The robot can save times, but it can also result in a lag, It is a machine so you can't expect too much from them, If the robot has malfunctioned, you need extra time to fix it, which would require reprogramming, If robots would do all the work, and the humans will just sit and monitor them, health hazards will increase rapidly, Obesity will be on top of the list and less labour at workplaces.

3. Increasing training expense

Whilst industrial robots are excellent for performing many tasks, as with any other type of technology, they require more training and expertise to initially set up. The expertise of a good automation company with a support package will be very important. To minimise your reliance on automation companies you can train some of your engineers on how to program robots, but you will still need the assistance of experienced automation companies for the original integration of the robot.

In recent years the number of industrial robots and the applications they can be used for has increased significantly. However, there still are some limitations in terms of the type of tasks they can perform, which is why we suggest that an automation company looks at your requirement to assess the options first. Sometimes a bespoke automated system may give a better or faster result than a robot. Also, a robot does not have everything built into it, often the success or failure of an industrial robotic system depends on how well the surrounding systems are integrated e.g. grippers, vision systems, conveyor systems etc. Only use good trusted robot integrators to be sure of the optimum results if you do choose to use industrial robots.

CHAPTER VIII

The relationship between social change and human behavior

Human Behavioral network job brings social economic benefits

What does human network job mean ? Why may human network job be popular? Why human network job behavior may influence economy ? Nowadays internet is popular to use. We can apply internet to find data , search any new things, even earn money. Why does internet may become huma network job source. For example, e-publish may be one kind of new human network job. Any authors may apply internet channel to help them to sell electronic or paper books from e-publisher web store. They may apply facebook, you tub etc. any online channel to promote themselves new books to let new readers to know whether when they may buy themselves favourable new topic books to read from electronic publisher web store.

Thus, future electronic publisher industry may help any authors to build internet network platform to help them to sell and promote ot advertise their any one new electronic or paper book topic to let global any one reader to choose to buy their any new topic books from electronic publisher web store easily and conveniently. However, it implies that electronic network platform author may be one kind of future new human network job in our societies.

How electronic network platform author job may bring economy benefit in macro economy view? A person can have few friends, contacts and still be very influential if these few friends and contacts are themselves highly influential, e.g. one author must not need to know any one reader in global society. When they like to choose any electronic books from electronic internet network platform. They may become the author's any one topic book buyer, when they feel the author's any one topic book is fun and attract they make decision to buth the strange author whose the topic book from electronic book publisher's platform web store conventiently in short time. Although, they are strangers, they do not know themselves , but the reader can understand what it way that made Google from writing platofrm to create new creative mind and typing network job method to replace traditional hand writing book method for global authors. It will be one kind of new human network writing job.

Hence, global any one reader can apply an innovative search engine , such as google.com to find whether whom author personal new topic books are value to read from internet.

Then, the electroniuc publisher's web store may be new book store platform sale network to help the author to sell many electronic or paper books from electronic network platform

in short time. So, internet may be future new network plaform to help global any one author to create network writing job absolutely. Furthermore, internet may be popular social media

to help any one author to build goold relationship between his/her readers. It is one kind of new network, human network job. New authors do not need to buy many paper books to prepare to put in any one book shop warehouse. Their every book can print on demand to reduce out of book stock in any one book shop. They may choose to sell either electronic books or paper books both from any one book publisher web store. So, electronic network platform may be one kind of good writing channel to help human authors to create income and it can also help authors to bring new creative mind and new topic fun content books to let readers to know and buy to read from electronic publisher network platform.

Why does human behavior may be one kind of new human network job to bring global economic advantages. ALthough, it may be free income or without inocme, but the person does the network behavior, his/her behavior may be bring advantages to influence many other people's health. For this case, when a worker in a coffee shop in an airport gets a vaccination aganinst the flu, it does not only helps him or her stay healthy, but also helps the many travellers who might otherwise have been inflected if that workers caught the flu. So, the externality , the result implies the vaccination of even a part of a community conveys benefits to the whole community. For example, governments pay special attention to the vaccinations of school children, teachers, health mothers, and the elderly, categories of people particularly susceptible not only to catching, but also to transmitting a disease.

It is not accidential that governments are heavily involved with vaccination . When there are externalities, free market, fail to persuade

individual incentives with society's
their the worker's decision of whether to get a vaccine ends up attracting whether other people get sick. The workers might not fully take all these other people's potential suffering into account when making her or his vaccination decision.

As Stanford University does many suggestions, understand this and tries to help them make the right decisions and so providers free flu vaccines for its staff and students.
Small pockets of unvaccinated individuals can allow a disease to gain a spread more widely well-being. For example, parent weighing the costs and benefits of a vaccine for their child is not always thinking of the consequences of that vaccination to other people. THese are markets in which subsidizing or regulating behavior can make everyone better off. Because the reason for requiring that a child be vaccinated before enrolling in school is not just to protect that child, because each child's vaccination affects others via potential contagions.

Robots take our jobs behavioral and economy influences

Robot job behavior brings economy influences

If one day robots can replace human to do simple, even complex jobs. They will bring what influences to our global societial economy.The popular economic refrain declares that the
global middle class is dying and robots will soon take our jobs, e.g. shopping center customer service jobs, library service jobs, cinema ticket sale jobs, restaurant kitchen cooker jobs,
even, bus drivers, taxi drivers etc. public transport driving jobs, accountant, doctors etc. professional jobs. Whether it is beautiful or petty matter if our future societies have many human jobs can be replaced to do from robots. Businessman must may reduce to employ employees and reduce to pay salary or wage, when robots can be replaced to do their employees tasks. But, societies must bring unemployement rate rises , due to societies will have many people loss jobs when their employers choose to buy robots to serve their clients or do any office tasks or customer service or cleaning etc. tasks.

In micro economy view, employers may save money in long term, but in macro economy view, it will cause unemployment ratio rises , even crime rate rises when there are many people lose
jobs in societies. These models of doom, though, fail to account for the

hundreds of businesses riding the waves of change in their industries when robots may be invented to replace human to do many simple , even complex tasks in our future societies.

WE may image that one small factory needs to manufacture fishes canes to sell to supermarket, the small , cheaper stuff and higher margin parts of the fishes manufacture industry. Before, this factory needs to employe many human factory workers need to help every fresh customer makeing the perfect fishing gear, designed for performance, durability, and cost in order to achieve to manufacture every fish cane in whole fished processing manufacturing stages. Every worker needs to spend about 15 to twenty minutes to finish every fish cane , till to delivery to any supermarket to sell. If this fish canes manufacturing factory can apply manufacturing robots to help them to finish any one working tasks , every robot can only spend five minutes to finish whole fresh fish cane manufacturing process. Thus, every robot can

help this factory save 10 to 15 minutes time to finsh every fish cane manufacturing process. IN fact, time is money, because when every robot can help this factory to reduce 10 to 15 minutes time to compare human worker. Then, this factory can finish about 20 fish canes in one hour if it can use robot to help it to manufacture fish canes. Otherwise, if this factory still use human workers to help it to manufacture fish canes, then it can finsh about 3 to 4 fish canes in one hour. SO, the manufacturing efficiency ensures that robots must help this fish manufacturing factory to raise fish canes number more than human workers. So, in robotic behavioral economy view, manufacturing robots must help this fish canes manufacturing factory to raise fish canes manufacturing number and deliver increasing number to supermarkets to prepare to sell every day. Robots can help this fish canes manufacturing factory bring manufacturing time saving, rising manufacturing efficiency, improving performance and reducing wages expenditure long time advantages in micro economy view. However, manufacturing robots can also bring disadvanages to society, e.g. increasing uncmployment ratio, increasing crime rate,

this factory workers will lose jobs and income, they need carn social welfare from government and increasing government finance pressure in short time, even long time in macro economic view.

Stanford University graduate program in economics, Scott lecturer explained that "in demand and supply economic theory for robots supply and demand case, robots supply number increasing may influence human workers demand number decrease. It sometimes calls " the efficient frontier".

No specific human beings were mentioned in any of economics classes. As robots supply and demand in market case, They (robots) may be purely theoretical " agents" who reached to the most reasonable sale prices in order to persuade any one businessman buyer to make manufacturing robot buying decision whether robots can help him / her to bring how much saving time , saving money, saving cost, improving performance, efficiency economic benefit before he/she plans to reduce workers number when he/she decides to apply robots to replace human workers in his/her factory or office or any service department, e.g. cinema ticket sale service, shopping center customer service, shopping center cleaning , supermarket customer service etc. service or sale tasks. When robots can replace human to do any one of these tasks in any organizations. So, robots may be human worker agents who reached to prices the way robots would react to a software command. There was nothing that explained why some people thrived and others did n't or why truly brilliant, hardworking people could fail when much lazier folks succeeded." Having been admitted to the Stanford University graduate program in economics, Scott lecturer hoped to get his answers there.

How robots influence our future social changing? Using the right technology can be a boon to your business in this economy. For internet example, it is easier than ever to find well-matched customers all around the world, to stay in contact with them, and to more quickly design the products they want. If you focus solely on being cutting -edge, though you risk letting the technology

take over what should be very robust relationships with your customers , employees, and colleagues. IN nowaddays society, technoligical advances and cutomation, personal

relationships in business are more crucial than ever. I mean that robots can not replace human to serve clients to let them to feel more comfortable and passion more easily. For shoe shop case example, if the shoe shop apply one robot to serve its clients to replace human shoe salesperson to serve its shoe customers. Robots ensure that they can not persuade every shoe potential buyer to make shoe buying decision more easily when robots need to contact every shoe potential buyer The reason is simple, because robots can not touch any one shoe buyer individual emotion very easier.

If the shoe buyer needs the robots to help him/her to choose any right

shoe styles when he/she can not feel himself / herself can make the most right shoe style choice decision. The robots can not replace human shoe salesperson to make shoe style choice judgement more easily. They must need longer time to analyze whether which shoe style may be the most suitable to the shoe buyer. Otherwise, human shoe salesperson may attempt to make the most right shoe style choice decision to help any one shoe buyer to chooce the most right style shoe because he/she owns shoe style sale experience, shoe style knowledge, the most important reason is that they can feel every shoe customer individual emotion to touch whether he/she will feel comfortable or happy when they attempt to help every shoe customer to seek the most right shoe style in every shoe customer whole shoe searching processing. Othwerwise, serving robots are only one machine, they can not touch or feel every shoe customer individual emotion whether he/she feel comfortable or unhappy or happy when they need to contact them in whole shoe searching processing. Hence, I believe that some tasks robots can
not repalce human staff to do very easily. Otherwise, robots may bring disadvanatges to let any one businessman to loss his/her customers, due to robots can not touch every customer
emotion to compare human staff in service tasks more easily. Robots serving customer behaviors may cause money lose and customers number lose to the shop in micro economic view.

Intellectual human economic behaviors

What does intellectual human economic behaviors mean ? I believe that when we choose or decide to do intellectual behaviors, then our societies will be influenced to bring economic growth in consequence.I shall attempt to indicate pollution case to explain how and why eithet our intellectual or foolish behaviors may bring economic growth or recession in consequence as below:

On one hand, for air pollution social case aspect example, if we only consider to buy cars to drive for working aimr or holiday leisure aim. Then, our societies air will be polluted. Our health will be influenced to bad. Our car driving behaviors may cause global environment air pollution serously. In long tiem, global air pollution will bring our bodies health to be bad. Although, ourselves car driving behaviors may bring our driving travelling leisure enjoyment and comfortable feeling in short time, also we so not need to pay public transport fare often, but we need to compensate ourselves health economic intangible loss due to air pollution , when cars number increases, dirty air will cause ouselves health to become bad.

In the result, we will need to pay more medical expenditure when we are old age, due to ourselves bodies will become bad, due to we breathe global dirty air every day, due to ourselves cars pollute air in long time, e.g. 10 to 20 years, even 30 more without limited air pollution environment. So, driving cars behavior may be one kind of human foolish behavior and our foolish behavior may bring ourselves future long time medical expenditure absolutely.

One the other hand, water pollution social aspect, if we often keep much rubblish to pollute sea, oil exploration porcessing pollute ocean , ships gas pollute ocaen, then fishes will eat polluted food and drive dirty water, due to global ocean is polluted.

In fact, because human only to conside how to buy boats to carry on leisure enjoyment activities, or catch cruises to travel on the sea. Also, oil manufacturers only consider researching anywhere to find new oil exploration places to manufacture oil product, when their oil exploration processes pollute ocarn . Consequently, global fishes drink polluted warer or eat polluted food. They will have poison. SO, human will have high chance to eat poison polluted fishes, due to fishes are poison or are polluted. So, human is doing foolish activities, we only hope to find oil exploration places to pollute ocean or we only spend money to buy ticket to catch ships to travel anywhere in global ocean. All of these human foolish behaviors will bring pollution to global ocean. On consequently, we will need to compensate to eat polluted or dirty or poision fishes, ourselves bodies health will be bad. In long time, we need have high chance to pay medical expenditure when we are old. So, pollution case may be one good example to explain how and why human foolish behavior may influence ourselves future need to compensate serious medical loss.

All of these human foolish behavior will bring pollution to global ocean. On consequently, we will need to compensate to eat polluted or dirty or poison fished , ourselves bodies health will be bad. In long time, we will have high chance to pay medical expenditure, when we are old. So, pollution case may be one good example to explain how and why human ourselves intellectual or foolish behaviors may influence future long time economic loss or economic growth or recession in micro and micro economic view.

On another water pollution aspect hand, if we often keep rubbish to sea, oil exploration processing pollutes ocean and ships' gas pollute ocean, then fishes will eat polluted food and drink dirty water, due to fishes will eat polluted food and drink dirty sea water because the global ocean is polluted seriously.

In fact, because human only consider how to buy boats to carry on any leisure water activities, or catches cruises to travel on the sea. Also, oil manufacturers only consider any where to find oil exploratin places to manufacture oil products from ocean, when their pol exploration processes can plooute ocean. Consequently, global fishes drink polluted water or eat direty food. They will have poison. So, human will have high chance to eat poison fishes.

Otherwise, such as pollutin case, it can infuence inflation or deflation. Consequently, the reason indicates supply and demand theory. If air pollution is serious, then we will consider health issue, global cars demand number may be influenced to reduce, when global cars number demand will reduce, global car prices and supply number will need to change to fall down in order to attract or persuade global car consumers choose to make car purchase decision.

Hence, global car manufacture number and car price will be influenced to reduce, due to global air pollution issue. Consequently, deflation will occur because when the country citizen usually does not spend much extra saving money to buy car expensive goods. Money value will be low. Otherwise, if global cair pollution is not serious, human considers to buy cars to enjoy driving leisure lives. So, global car demand is influenced to increase , also global car price will also influenced to increase.

Consequently, gobal human will choose to buy cars to drive. Due to we accept to spend extra saving to buy expensive car goods. Car sale price and supply may be influenced to rise up. Money value is influenced to reduce. Inflation may be influenced, due to global car consumers number increases, we would not have extra money to spend easily. Car expensive goods expenditure influences our spending habit to avoid to make car purchase decision more easily. So, human intellectual or foolish activities may bring inflation or deflation consequency in possible indirectly in macro economic view.

On conclusion, above pollution case explain that how and why human intellectual or foolish economic behaviors may bring inflation or deflation consequency as wll as economic growth or recession consequency as well as any goods demand and supply increasing or decreasing consequency. It implies that human behavior may have indirect relationship to influence any goods demand and supply number to either increase or decrease result as well as any goods price will be influenced to increase or decrease in micro and macro economic view.

The relationship between social change and human behavior

Why does economic changes may influence human individual behavioral change? I shall attempt to indicate shopping behavior and staying at home behavior to explain their case and effect relationsip as below:

Human behavior can be influenced by economic change or economic change can be influenced by human behavior? Why does recession may influence consumers reduce shopping desire? In social recession suitation, it is possible that many people lose jobs suddenly, due to businessmen lose many customers. They need to make decision to reduce employees number in order to continue to keep businesses. Consequently, many firms (organizations) their employees may lose jobs. When they have much time, due to lose jobs, they will feel to avoid to spend too much time and money to go to shopping often. Many losing jobs people, they will often stay at homes. So, they will reduce time to go to shopping, then non essential products won't their preferable choice purchase products. Hence, recession will change many losing jobs people their shopping or consumption desires to avoid to buy non essential products often . Usually when economic boom, many people have jobs to do because consumers number must increase when many people have jobs to do. Then, many people can accept to spend money to buy non essential products often. Many people feel spend time to go to shopping can satisfy their purchase of any kinds of new products useful psychology or desire. So, recession is one good example to explain it can influence many people do not like often to leave homes to go to shopping easily. Many people like to stay at homes, becaue they feel worry about spending too much shopping time when they leave homes. Their staying home time is one good negative shopping behavior example. So, economic change may influence human individual behavior changes , they have direct cause and efect relationship in behavioral economic view.

May human behavior influence economic change? Is it possible that human behavior may bring the country social economic change in macro economic or micro behavioral economic view ? I shall indicate publishing industry example. Do you feel that if there are many students feel learning is very important when they read many books or many of students feel interesting to read or they have reading new books in habit, then it is possible that the country will have many students like to spend time to go to any book shops to choose the books, they feel that they can help they learn new knowledge.

Then the country will increase students number, they often spend time to visit any one book shop every week. Their visiting book shops behavior which may become their habits. So, the country will increase students number, they often spend time to visit book shops. Also, it implies that visiting book shops behaviors may be their behavioral habits.

So, when the country has many students often spend time to visit book shops , their visiting book shops behaviors may help any one book shop to raise books sale chance. So, the country's student individual often visiting book shop behaviors, their habitual visiting book shops behaviors must may assist help any one book shop to increase books sale number absolutely.

Consequently, any one book shop , its books sale humber must be influenced to increase to increase because the country will have many students like or feel need visit book shops habit in order to choose any suitable books to buy to read at home in order to raise themselves learning effort. When the country has many bok shops often have many students visit their book shops, then their books sale number may be influenced to increase. It explain why student individual visiting book shop behavior may help any one book shop sale number increases also.

How human productive behavior may influence economic development

May any country which citizen behavior assist themselves country development? It is one cause and effect economic question. I mean that if the country itself citicen can not concentrate mind or energy to choose to do one kind of industry in order to let themselves country can bring the most benefit, then whether the counry itself economy can bring the most serious economic benefit. I shall attempt to indicate these countries themselves indistry choice to explain whether these countries themselves citizen productive behavior may help themselves countries to achieve the largest economic benefits. I shall indicate as below:

New Zealand farmer individual wine productive behavior

For New Zealand country example, this country concerns itself effort is foucs on farming agricultural aspect. So, this country has many farmers concentrate on farming agricultural aspect. May New Zealanders choose to spend time to produce different kinds of wines, e.g. wine or red grape wine is for the people are eating meat, or they are eating dinner.

When these New Zealanders their behaviors choose to do farming or agriculture to grow and produce different kinds of taste of white or red grape wine drinking products job. Themselves grape agriculture behavior will influence these New Zealanders themselves, they can learn how to improve different kinds of grape wine drinking products in order to achieve every kinds of white or read grape wines taste improving aim during their white or red grape producing process.

Why can New Zealander every individual white or read grape wine producers improve their white or read grape wine taste more easily? In behavioral economic view, it can explain that why any one New Zealander white or read grape wine producer can be encouraged or excited or persuaded to concentrate nervous and energy and effort to learn how to improve their white or red grape wine products easily.

In fact, New Zealand is one agricultural food export country. It has good natural environment resource , e.g. land, seed to provide any one farmer to produce themselves any kinds of agricultrual food products, e.g. fruit, or wine food products. Because New Zealanders know themselves country has enough natural resource . So, in common, many New Zealanders choose to attempt to do farming agricultural jobs in order to export themselves any kinds of fruit or meat or wine products to overseas or sell to domestic in order to earn profit.

So, when these New Zealand farmers number has been increasing every year. This country farmers will feel themsleves competition between this New Zealand farmers themselves are serious due to they may feel New Zealanders choose to do agriculture businesses in order to export themselves different kinds of farming food to overseas or sell to local to earn profit.

Hence, when many New Zealand farmers feel that farmers number has been increasing every year. They will feel themselves competition is serious. They must need to spend much time and nervous and effort to research what method is the best how to produce the best taste of white or red grape wine products in order to let local or overseas wine buyers to choose to buy his/her producing white or read grpae products to drink.

Hence, in competition psychological view, may influence many New Zealand white or reaad wine producers had been beginning to change their learning behavior on researching what method is the best in order to produce the best quality of taste red or white wine products to sell in order to attract overseas or local white or read grape wine drinkers to choose to buy his/her wine products. Their behavior will focus on learning how to raising or improving white or read grape wine taste method more than only focus on producing a large number white or red grape wine products. They believe wine quality is more important to compare wine producing number.

So, New Zealand wine producers themselves wine producers behaviors have been changing on concentrating on researching wine quality method aspect more then wine producing number aspect in behavioral economic view.

America high technological productive behavior

For America example, US is one high technological country, it owns many high technological knowledge talent inventors, e.g. computer science inventors. Hence, US must attract many diferent countries owning high technological computer inventors choose to go to US to develop their computer science profession career. Also, it seems that when many computer science inventors or professions choose to go to US to develop themselves computer science new career. In behavioral economic view, due to their leaving themselves countries choice, which may bring influence themselve country job behaviors need to be changed. They must need to adapt US new live. Because they will forgive their past computer science job. These computer science professionals need to spend time to adapt US new lives. They " past computer science job behaviors" will need to be changed to their new US any computer employer's new computer science job model.

Because their traditional computer science jobs needed to be forgot in their themselves countries. They will feel their old computer science job knowledge and behavior needed to change in order to let their US any one new of computer company employer feels satisfactory to accept their new working behavior in any one US computer organization.

So, on the other hand, many US computer company employer will feel that they must need time to accept any one new overseas computer science professions their working behaviors, their working attitude daily, because these foreign comouter science professional, their past computer working behaviors and working attitude must be different to US domestic computer science professions.

In behavioral economic view, these overseas computer science professions, their working behaviors and attitude must be needed to change in order to adapt any one US new computer company itself domestic or local computer science professional stafs themselves daily working behaviors and attitude because these overseas and local computer science professionals must need to team work together.

In behavioral economic view, it is only one way that foreign computer science professionals must need to change themselves past country traditiona daily working behaviors and attitude in order to cooperate with these US local computer science professionals in teams more easily.

Consequently, if these foreign compute science professionals can change their past working behaviors and attitude to let any one US local computer science professional feels to cooperate with them easily in short time. Then, the US computer company itself whole computer professional teams themselves efficiencies will be influenced to raised or improved by the changing past working attitude and working behaviors of these foreign computer science professionals. So, in behavioral economic view, only if US any one computer company hopes itself computer teams themselves efficiency can be raised or improved when it decides to employ foreign computer science professionals and US domestic computer science professionals. They need to work in teams together. They must need to let these foreign computer science professionals to know how to change their working behaviors and attitude to let their domestic computer science professionals feel easy to work together. Then, the US computer company itself whole team efficiency must be rasied or improved easily in short time.

- China share market investing behavior

For China share market example, economic development depends on financial market. Because if many Chinese have interest to invest to carry on shares buying and selling activities in orde to learn how to earn shares interest and share profit when the China shareholder can make decision to sell himself/herself shares in the the high price, then he/she can earn money when he/she can sell the China company's shares in the high sale share price position.

If China has many Chinese like to spend time to carry on investing shares activities. Themselves shares buying and selling behaviors will influence China has many companies can increase fund from many Chinese shareholders in order to have enough money to expand or develop themselves businesses in China in long term.

Consequently, when China can have many Chinese like to attempt to carry on buying and selling shares investing behaviors in China share market. Themselves buying and selling shares behaviors can help many Chinese companies have effort to increase enough money or capital in order to continue to do their businesses in long term absolutely. So, it explains why when many Chinese become shareholders , they can assist China will have many companies continue to develop their businesses if many Chinese like to carry on shares buying and selling investing behaviors in long time in

China financial investment market nowadays in behavioral economic view.

Why has any individual country have many people invest share behavior which can influence the country's macro consumption desire?

I shall apply shares market buying and selling investment behavior to explaiin why shares investment behavior which may impact the country's overal consumption desire as below:

In behavioral economic view, I assume that when the coutry has many people have interest to attempt to carry on shares buying and selling investment behavior, then their frequent shares buying and selling behaviors which may bring negactive consumption desire or shopping desire of these shares investors their consumer behavior.

The reason is simple, when the country has many share buyers number suddenly been increasing rapidly. Consequently, these large group share investors must need to spend much time to research any kinds of company shares variations, whether when their share prices will rise up of fall down in order to achieve buying the company's shares in the lowest price and selling the company's shares in the highest price level in order to earn profit.

Basic on this reason, they must need to spend much extra time to research share prices changing behavior every day, e.g. one working person will wait to leave his/her job, after he/she can spend time to gather data to research the day's share price changing behavior after dinner. So, the working person's right time may be his/her share price market research behavior. Before he/she may spend his/her night time to go to shopping after dinner, but nowadays, he/she will fogive to do his/her shopping behavior before dinner or after dinner at hight sometime. He/she will make decision to spend much night time to turn on computer to click on share market website to research his/her share purchase choice to investigate whether his/her share price whether it rises up or falls down at the moment in order to make his/her share buying or selling decision at ever night time.

I mean the when the country has many people are share investors, their shares investment behavioral spenging time which will influence many shops lose customers at might often because the country will have many people feel need to spend night time to turn on computer or watch television to investigate share price variation. So, the country will have many people / share investors choose to stay at home in order to carry on share price variation investigation behavior, they need to listen share market update news from radios or watch the share market update news

from computer or TV at home every night. Consequenly, they must reduce times to leave themselves homes at night. So, their shopping behavior also will be reduced. Because these share investors feel need to spend time to investigate share price variation news at homes which can bring economic benefits (high opportunity benefits) when they choose to forgive to leave homes to go to shopping times (opportunity cost) every night.
On conclusion, it seems that when the country has many people are share investors, then their share price investigating behavior may bring negative shopping emotion at night. Consequently, the country's any one shop may lose many customers from this share investor consumer group in behavioral economic view. Hence, when the country's share investors number had been increasing rapidly, it will influence any shops lose many customers from this share investing customer group at night frequenly in short time, even long time in behavioral economic view, because their shopping desires or shopping emotion will be brought negative feeling when they make decisions to spend much time to listen radios or watch TV or computers share price update nes at night. Hence, share market will bring negative impact to influence consumer shopping desire or negative shopping emotion in behavioral economic view.

Can technology influence human shopping behavioral change?
Nowadays, technological development has reached mature stage, whether technological mature stage may bring positive or negative shopping emotion influence to global consumers. I shall aplly internet inventin or ecommerce shopping channel tool to explain whether internet technology can bring postive or negative influence to global consumer behavior in behavioral economic view.
Internet is a good technological tool, it brings e-commerce business chance. In fact, commonly, global has have many businessmen choose to use internet channel to carry on their products transactions between global online-buyers and their electronic websites. So, global many shoppers had begun to feel online shopping is more convenient to compare visiting shops shopping. Their shopping behaviors have been changed from internet technological tool. Global has many shoppers choose to buy any products from any overseas or local businessmen their web stores. They only need to spend time to find any businessmen their webstores to choose the most suitable products to pay visa to buy from their webstores. at homes. So, in general, global had have may shoppers had changed their shopping

behaviors from visiting shops to visiting webstores at homes often.

So, it seems that internet technological tool had influenced global many shops disappear, but internet webstores will be replaced their actual shops on streets. Some of businessmen either they choose webstores to replace shops or choose websotes and shops both or still keep shops only. Hence, internet tool influences global businessmen have three kinds of products sale channels to let globa local and overseas consumers to choose how to buy their products.

However, in fact, many of global shoppers, youngers and olders had begun to accept to buy any products from webstores. They feel to spend time to leave homes to visit shops , their shopping behaviors will be wasted time to not essential part to their daily lives. Hence, since internet technological invention, it had changed many consumers their traditional visiting shops shopping habit to change to buying products from webstores channel.

However, on the one hand, internet creates webstores ecommerce shopping channel to let global many consumers do not need to leave homes to go to shopping. It brings negative visiting shops shopping emotion to global general consumers nowadays. But on the other hand, it also brings positive visiting internet webstores shopping emotion to global general consumer nowadays. So, it seems that global many consumers feel that they often do not need to spend much time to go out shopping. Many global consumers feel convenient and enjoy to choose any products to buy from different internet webstores, when the online buyer chooses the most suitable product, he she only needs to pay visa card to buy the product from the online seller's webstore conveniently at home.

Hence, online shopping can bring economic benefit to online buyers, e.g. avoiding walking time or spending transport fare to visit the shop to go to shopping, shortening or reducing shopping time to do another important matter.

On conclusion, global many consumers began feel online shopping can bring more economic benefits on shortening shopping time, avoiding transport fare spending aspect. So, online shopping will be popular shopping behavior for future long time. It may encourage global many shoppers can make rapid shopping decision in short time in order to carry on any products buying transaction to global any one online shopper in short time easily in behavioral economic view. So, global many businessmen had begun to build themselves one attraction webstore in order to persuade different countries consumers to choose to click themselves webstores from internet channel to buy any kinds of products in short time easily.

So, internet technology had changed consumers traditional shopping behaviors to build positive online shopping emotion as well as raise online sellers' any products sale chance easily in behavioral economic view.

Why and how human behavior may influence the country's economic growth or recession?

When one country has many people choose to do the same matter for one period, whether their behavior may influence the country's pvera; economic growth or recession . I shall attempt to indicate cases toexplain their relationship as below:

For flowing rubblish behavioral case example, do you feel that when the country has many people often flow rubblish on the streets, instead of their flowing rubblish behavior may bring streets dirty? But, their flowing rubblish behavior may explain that this country has people may have enough money to buy food to ear, or enough cloths to wear, enough bottles of water to drink, even they may have enough money to buy new television, radio, refrigeraters , washing machines, desktops or laptops electronic home products from old to new to use in order to satisfy their living needs. So, when they flow old electronic home products, their flowing old home electronic products behaviors may seem that they have enough money to buy other new home electronic products to replace old home electronic products to use at homes.

However, it seems thaat this country ought have many people have jobs to do. So, many of them, they can easy to make purchase decison to flow any old home electronic products and buy any new home electronic products to use . Because this country has many people have jobs to do. So, they can often not use old home electonic products to become rubblishs to flow on streets after they had bought any kinds of new home electronic homes.

In fact, it also implies that this country's economy grows rapidly. So, many businesses can glow up rapdly. When they expanded their businesses, they must need to increase employees number in order to let they help themselves to raise productivity or serve their clients absolutely. So, when the country has many businesses can grow up, it seems that its economy must be better or it is improved to compare past. Due to many different kinds of home electronic products had been often bought to use by this country people in this period. So, this country's any streets can be observed that expensive electronic home products were flowed on streets anywhere. then, this country will have many electronic home products sellers can sell their home electronic products very easily. When this country has many people can find any kinds of jobs to do easily. So, due to unemploymen rate had been decreasing.

In behavioral economic view, as this many electronic home products rubblish country case, we can observe this country may have many people have jobs to do. So, consumption number has been increased long time. So, cheap food, or expensive home electronic products may be rubblish on any streets. This country's people , their flowing rubblish behaviors may be explained that many of people have enough jobs to do, so they have ability to buy any good taste food to eat or buy any kinds of expensive electronic home products to use. So, this country's economy may be improved for this long period. So, in behavioral economic view, when this country can have many electronic home products rubblishs are flowed on anywherer in streets frequently. It seems that this country will have many people have jobs to do, so it causes they often change old home electronic products or replaced them easily, when they have enough income to spend to buy any kinds of new home electronic products to use at homes easily. Moreover, their flowing old electronic home products behaviors also indicate that this country has many people their salaries may be increased in possible from their emplyers. When this country can have many different kinds of home electornic products are sold. It means that this country's electronic home products needs or demand had been increasing, due to many people have jobs to do and income increases to excite their living of needs also improve. Consequently, this country may seem have better economic improvement. We can observe from this country's electronic home products rubblish increasing income in theis period.

On conclusion, this country ought experience economic growth at this period. So, " flowing expensive electronic home rubblish increasing number " may seem that this country's economic growth is rapidly in this period, due to many people have jobs to do as well as salaries increase in this period.

Technology how impacts human behavior changing?

Technology how influences human behavior to bring changing? For example, online share purchase and sale transaction from smart phone brings share investor can do share buying or selling transation in any where and any time conveniently, non manual driving auto vehicle, bring car owner feels comfortable and spends free time to do other matter, e.g. reading, listening mucis in himself or herself car freely. electrical energy vehicle can help car owner to reduce air polluton and it can brings the drivers do not feel drive long time in any journeys in order to avoid air pollution for environmental protection responsible car drivers in our societies. Thus, they will drive long time in any journeys when they can drive electronic energy cars to replace oil energy cars.

However, online technology can also bring consumers can choose to stay at homes to buy any things from seller individual online webstore conveniently. Such as online technology can bring shoppers do not need to spend much time to visit shops to buy any things. They can choose any kinds of products from any online sellers individual online webstores conveniently at homes. Online technology excite busy consumers can make purchase decision easily as well as it can help online sellers sell any kinds of products from internet easily.

In behavioral economic view, technology can change human behavior to be improved, it can let human feels comfortable, more free time ro use, rapid making any decisions, such as apply smart phones to make share purchase or sale transaction decision, online shopping decision, even travelling any where decision in short time, when the traveller finds the most cheap hotel accommodation room price and air ticket price frm any travel agent online tourism webstore, then the potential travel customer can follow the online hotel accommodation price and air ticket price data to make decision when to buy the air ticket from the airline travel agent or make decision when to prebook which hotel accommodation room to go to the country to travel from online travel agent tourism webstores. So, technology can encourage global any country travelers to make anywhere to trvel rapidly. If the traveler can find the country's general hotel rooms and airline tickets prices had been decreasing more sightly. The traveler may make travel decision to choose the country to travel in short time, then he/she can prebook the country;s any hotel room and airline ticket to pay by visa fraom the country's any hotel and airline travel agent webstores., before one week, even one month or more easily. Hence, online technology can also encourage traveler individual frequent travel times to be increased, due to global travelers can find any hotel rooms and airline tickets prices from internet conveniently at homes. They do not need to spend time to visit any airline travel agent to enquire travel choice country's hotel rooms prices and airline ticket prices. They can compare global travel of countries choices ' all hotels rooms and airline agents air tickets prices to make prebook airline seat and hotel room decision before one week, one month even six months

early.
On conclusion, online technology can encourage global travelers can make travelling any where and when traveling time desicions easily. It can excite tourism industry develops in long time. Also, such as electricity cars invention can encourage environment protection car owners do car purchase decision easily, because they can choose to drive electronic energy cars to replace oil energy cars in order to avoid air pollution occurs easily. So, electronic cars can increase electronic car purchasrs number, due to many of environmental protection attitude of car owners can choose to drive electricity cars to bring air cleans, even non -manual driving cars can encourage lazy driving and free time driving car owners to choose to buy non-manual (artificial intelligent) cars to drive , because they can spend much free time to read, listen music or do any matters in themselves cars, they do not need to drive cars, robotic (AI) auto driving machine is such one non-manual driver to help them to drive themselves cars confidently. So, non-manual driving cars can attract lazy and enjoying free time driving car owners to choose to buy to replace traditional manual cars to drive easily. Moreover, online share transaction can help any share investors to make share buying and selling decision in short time easily. When they can apply smart phones technological tool to carry on share buying and selling activities easily. They can observe any share rising or falling price suitation from smart phones in any where any any time easily. So, smart phone technology can help global any shareholders to make share purchase and sale transaction easily. So, technology can encourage human makes decision in short time rapidly.

www.ingramcontent.com/pod-product-compliance
Ingram Content Group UK Ltd.
Pitfield, Milton Keynes, MK11 3LW, UK
UKHW041639190726
13854UKWH00006B/2590

9 798888 151952